TALES FROM THE DAY

Life changing events that truth be told
all happened under the heading of "oops."

WAYNE D. MCFARLAND

Black Rose Writing | Texas

ISBN: 978-1-68433-124-6
PUBLISHED BY BLACK ROSE WRITING
www.blackrosewriting.com

Printed in the United States of America
Suggested Retail Price (SRP) $15.95

Tales from the Day is printed in Cambria

Praise for
TALES FROM THE DAY

McFarland is one helluva story teller - and a good guy to have along when you get thrown in jail.

—Mike Delaney, author *Cyclone Bobcat*

***

"In general, memoirs really suck," observes new author Wayne McFarland in the opening line of Tales From The Day. On the other hand, to savor this self-described "memoir of sorts" that begins in the mid-twentieth century is to feast on a remarkable array of first-person accounts served with the sensibilities of a seasoned novelist. McFarland combines astute observations, skilled storytelling, and a blend of amusement, self- awareness and candor that most of us couldn't muster even after years of therapy. You may alternate between "I wish I'd been there" and "I'm glad it was him and he lived to tell it." As the book wraps, McFarland muses that some tales still remain untold. Count me among the eager readers who look forward to the day he tells them.

—Bill Lenz, Writer, Producer, Director, Narrator; 4 time Cindy Award winner; 4 time Telly Award winner; 2 time Cine Golden Eagle Award winner; winner Grand Award and others

***

"...extremely well written. Read this book for pure fun and enjoyment. The stories are amazing and incredibly, all TRUE!"

—Steven Arenas, Emmy nominee. 21 years, TV animation. Director, major studio TV animation post production, 15 years.

***

"Wayne has a way of telling a true story that captivates and holds your attention. Can't put it down. Want to know what's next. This shows what an exciting life you can have if you try hard enough. Exciting, scary, hilarious and poignant.

—Richard Bultman, Attached To Army Intelligence (Cold war)

***

"Entertaining, funny and well written. Will Rodgers would be proud."

—Ken Bangs, author of *Guardians in Blue*

***

An apt title for this book would be Adventures of a Young Man. But alas, Hemingway has already gobbled that one up. Wayne McFarland's rollicking memoir reads like the autobiography of a mature Huckleberry Finn. This series of separate vignettes weaves into a narrative arc, that describes a number of humorous misadventures strewn along the pathway to maturity and ultimate success. The tales are all well-paced, brilliantly written, poignant, agonizing, funny and, in places, all-consuming. It is told with great verve, pluck and gusto. The rich metaphors and sometimes self- debasing similes produced peals of laughter in this hardened old combat soldier. Set largely in the 60's, any reader from boomer to millennial will find meaning in the life lessons imparted by this story. An excellent read.

—R. Bruce Logan, author, *Back to Vietnam: Tours of the Heart, Finding Lien*, and *As The Lotus Blooms*

***

"Tales from the Day" is a delight! A real gem! But, what really sets these stories apart is the refreshingly honest and unvarnished way in which the author explores both individuals and events. Each story skillfully details the remarkable, unique, and often humorous qualities of each character and how these relate to the circumstances in which they ultimately find themselves. "Tales from the Day" is a joy to read!... tremendously well written... story- telling at its best...I only hope that there is more to come . . .

—Steve Schultz, Ph.D., Professor of Chemistry/Chemistry Instructor Minnesota West Community and Technical College

***

DEDICATION

First and foremost, to my wife and best friend Gloria of course. Also to Curt Gudmundson who has been such a supporter and friend over the years, plus his wife Pam, a dear friend and supporter as well. Lastly, but not leastly, to those wonderful people Richard and Tracy Bultman.

TALES FROM THE DAY

CONTENTS

CHAPTER ONE

"When you put down the good things you ought to have done, and leave out the bad ones you did do; well, that's Memoirs" Will Rogers

In general, memoirs really suck.

This is not because they're badly written, which they often are, but because they're "me walls" in prose. It's an eye-roller that every aging "Honey I'm Home" product of returning soldiers post WW II now thinks the world is desperate to hear about How Life Was. Really, no one gives a crap.

One thing that always amuses me in "look back" works is how, in addition to a golden glow of What Never Really Was, many authors try to portray life's events as a quasi-planned, rather orderly progression of moments which taught Life Lessons. In reality, life is a delightful shit storm of random events, most of which are stumbled into, make little sense and teach Life Lessons in the same way one learns from getting hit with a board.

Yeah, this indeed is a memoir of sorts, if shark fishing in one's underwear, roping a bear, getting drunk with your Grandfather, or losing ten grand at the Hollywood Sign is a memoir. The Day Johnny Cash Hit On My Wife is on the roster as well, for the only name drop in all the stories. There's also a thing about getting shot in Arkansas and a road trip with a monkey.

I can't deny these were life shaping events, but truth be told they all happened under the heading of "oops."

Life lessons? Well, O.K. then, buckle up: here's a few for you. The first four were driven home during a summer's squat in the Idaho woods, 40 miles from anywhere.

Here's how you deal with loss—assuming you live in the woods by a river.

The Day We Roped The Bear

If we hadn't been so bored, I swear to you we would not have roped the bear.

I was 19 and grass green.

After shanghaiing a buddy, I had team hitched a couple of thousand miles to nail a summer job with the forest service. For reasons I cannot remember and cannot now comprehend, as a college kid, fighting forest fires in Idaho seemed like a damn fine idea. I was amply rewarded for my folly by being hired and banished to a line camp far and away in the Clearwater National Forest in northern Idaho where mostly we cut brush, poisoned tree cankers and spent occasional butt puckering days fighting lightning strike fires.

In those days anyway, summer Forest Service grunts slept in bunkhouses and ate at a communal mess, military style. My bunk mates were an eclectic bunch: a coal miner from Virginia escaping a shotgun wedding, and, among others, a Nez Perce kid who swore he was related to Chief Joseph (related or not, he had both a lazy grin and a cousin scarred from hairline to chin who staggered in one night, produced a rifle and announced he was going to kill us all).

Filling out my roommate roster was a grizzled old guy with ropy muscles who never talked except to mutter "college shitheads," and a sprinkling of other college kids along with a few itinerant hobos; just out of jail types who never seemed to stick more than a week or two.

The first person I met in my summer bunkhouse home was Ervie, the "college shithead" guy; a knurled dwarf of an old Mountain Man (or so he seemed to me then). I stuck out my hand. He stuck up his face. "Listen you college fuck, keep the hell away from me." The second person, Tim, was a rangy lad from Oklahoma. His claim to fame was he could play guitar a little, sing like Caruso and was screwing the only woman within fifty miles of our camp. On hearing this, I opined his True Name was really The Golden Grub, which over his on-going, pissed off objections stuck to him like glue thereafter. The Grub became my Bear Roper Partner.

Nobody gave much of a damn what anyone else did except when it came to the actual work. Camp rules were that no one went out by themselves on a project. Getting hurt alone back in the bushes could get you killed so every job had at least two people on it. Our Ranger, Bob, who led our motley camp had no sense of humor at all. Worse yet, he knew damn well how much work should be done in a day whether it was by two men or ten. The formula was pretty simple: if Ranger Bob decided someone was screwing off, the errant members of that particular crew were immediately assigned every crap job which came down the pike. There were a hell of a lot of those, some involving actual crap.

So there you have it: mostly hard, physical labor filled weekdays, followed by empty hours in the evening and long weekends—what could you do Friday night, Saturday and Sunday in the woods in a forest line camp full of guys after all? Occasionally we could go in to the booming metropolis of Orofino, Idaho, but after I was given a couple of bunkhouse lessons in how to shoot craps and lost all my money plus one future paycheck, that was really not an option. The Grub, an inveterate gambler, had not fared much better, so mostly on evenings and weekends it was the two of us sitting around wishing we either had better sense or better luck.

I swear to you, The Grub started the whole thing. "So," he says to me one day, "on a scale of one to 10 how bored are you?"

We knew that bears hung out at the garbage pit; four black bears. And there were only two bear trails leading in and out of the dump, so we figured setting up an ambush would be a no brainer. The Grub maintained he had done all the intel required by watching these bears on many boring evenings and chucking dirt clods at them to make sure that the bears ran away from rather than, with mayhem on their minds, towards humans.

Vastly reassured, I stole some thick rope from the "hot shot" helicopter kit. The Grub procured, from God knows where, a railroad tie.

One early, weekday evening, we tied one end of the rope around the railroad tie and looped the other end, tied into a lasso, over what we had determined was the bear exit trail from the dump (later, in the aftermath, the Grub and I agreed that we really should've waited till the weekend to conduct the Great Bear Rope).

Hiding in the bushes, we were gratified to see all four bears arrive at the dump right on schedule for their evening snack. The Grub gave the signal, a piercing, warbling whistle alerting the bears, Ranger Bob and our bunkmates that something was amiss. This was definitely a tactical error in our war plan. We leaped up shouting and hurling dirt clods, both to not hurt the bears (as we later maintained), but in truth mostly not to piss them off by throwing rocks. The Bears thundered down the exit path and right through our lasso-- one, two, three, gone. Number four we nailed: the rope caught him around his head and his front leg for a perfect catch.

We now had successfully executed our plan; we had roped a bear...now what the hell were we going to do with it?

The bear obligingly solved the problem for us.

Squalling at the top of its lungs, it climbed right straight up a huge, tall tree, lifting that heavy, tar laden railroad tie an easy five feet up off the ground...and that tie was really, really heavy. Looking towards our bunkhouse, we can see our bunkmates spilling out like gophers from a hole and heading in our direction, closely followed by Ranger Bob carrying a gun and a very grim expression.

So, being 19 years old (well okay, The Grub was 20) the only hope of salvation we could think of was to pull the squealing bear out of the tree. Yes, we panicked I suppose, but then if you have never heard a bear yowling in distress you simply cannot imagine the decibel level or the horrifying, chalkboard sound. So I hopped up and grabbed the railroad tie while The Grub seized the rope, both of us heaving mightily downwards at the same time.

The result was similar to pulling the chain on an old-fashioned, overhead toilet. The bear, feeling the pull of the rope, immediately pissed all over us. A copious bear bucket of warm pee was immediately followed by a huge load of ursine crap, all of which, heartily assisted by gravity, unerringly found us as we stood at the base of the tree. Looking up.

Ranger Bob and our laughing-to-tears bunk mates arrived just in time to find us soaking wet from the bear shower and reeking of scat, glumly staring at the tree where the bear, still howling, had now moved to the very top, tangling the rope in branch after branch. I recall Ranger Bob fingering his rifle, a puny little thing, 22 caliber, (how are you going to kill the bear with that? I remember thinking) while slowly looking up at the bear and then back to us.

Finally after a long, drawn out silence he spoke: "I am just trying to decide who to shoot."

They finally had to cut the tree down. The bear rode it all the way to the ground emitting a cartoon like "Yaaaaaaa" sound. It bounced once when it hit the (fortunately) soft earth, threw off the rope and ran after its companions who by now were long gone.

We of course never lived it down, although the story told in raucous detail by our bunk mates was always good for a few free beers for us so I suppose the episode had its merits. Ranger Bob made good on his reputation by assigning us to every rotten job to be performed for the balance of the summer. We did them cheerfully while counting ourselves lucky, which undoubtedly we were.

As the sun set on that fateful day, walking back to the

bunkhouse I saw Ranger Bob sitting on the bank of the Snake River which ran furiously along the edge of our camp. His rifle lay beside him. Being too inexperienced to leave well enough alone, I walked up to him and asked if he minded if I asked him a question.

He didn't look up, just kept staring at the river. "Go ahead."

"Isn't that rifle a .22?" I asked. "Can you really stop a bear with that thing? It's kind of small, isn't it?"

A pause. "I had a lot of guns a year ago," he responded, almost as if I wasn't there. "Some of them were big enough to stop an elephant. I threw all my guns in the river."

We were running out of light and I had run out of gas, so showing more brains than I had all day I didn't say anything and just sat down on the riverbank. Besides I had no idea at all as to how to respond. Threw all his guns in the river?

"She was a lot younger than me and people said it would never last... but I did love her so. One day I caught her with a guy, a younger guy. I knew him. I liked him. By the time I got my gun out of the case and loaded they were both gone. I never saw either one of them again."

"I never wanted to do anything more in my life than kill them both. So I threw all my guns in the river. After a while I didn't want to kill them anymore."

By now darkness had descended, the total, inky blackness that only night in the deep forest can produce. We both got up and went our separate ways, he to the Ranger's cabin and I to the bunkhouse. Ranger Bob and I saw each other every day thereafter during the course of the summer. We never spoke of that day or that evening, ever.

CHAPTER TWO

"Drunk people suck when they're not me" Author unknown

At the time I worked on a fire crew in the Idaho forest, it was a men only deal. Women obviously did not and do not have the physical stamina to engage in heavy exercise. Just look at the World Champion, US Women's Soccer team, or the women's Olympic downhill skiing team for example.

Back then, the resulting "no women allowed" gravel piles of man crews led to a lot of public gas passing, and a quasi-social rule that acceptable venting was beating the snot out of someone. Or worse.

Dealing with loss by throwing a few thousand dollars' worth of guns in the river was one forest lesson.

Here's another: stick together in times of trouble and stay the hell away from a mean drunk.

The Day Kenny's Cousin Tried To Kill Us All

Along with our team-mates, Kenny and I fought forest fires in the Clearwater National Forest in northern Idaho. Mid-summer, after a big fire, Kenny told me his real name was Little Bear and gave me an "Indian name" which he pronounced "Ma-coom-sqway." I only later found out it meant "dirty shorts."

Kenny swore he was the Great Grandson of the famous Nez

Perce leader Chief Joseph.

Chief Joseph was a war leader. A reluctant war leader, whose tactics are still studied in War Colleges. When the US government decided to steal the Nez Perce lands too, he counseled peace, but war came anyway. In 1877, outnumbered 10 to 1, he led a band of men, women, and children 1,700 miles. It was a multi-month, desperate run to freedom in Canada. But, 64 miles from safety, it fell to him at the Montana Bear Paw mountains to surrender his people. That day he said "...My heart is sick and sad. From where the sun now stands, I will fight no more, forever". He died in exile in 1904, on a reservation far from home. He was 64 years old when, his doctor said, he died of a broken heart. (1)

"His real name was Hinmatóowyalahtqit (Hin-mah-too-yah-lat-kekt)" Kenny told me one day, shortly after we met. "He was named Chief Joseph by white pieces of shit."

"Like you," he added.

He and I were bunkmates of sorts in a five-man, open bunkhouse bay. Initially, only two of the other beds on our five-bunk floor were occupied. One was filled by an older, ox-like guy, Ervie, who collected big tree Burls in order to hand-carve canes. He fiercely hated all college kids. The other bed was occupied by an on the run Virginia coal miner, Victor. One chaser, he said, was his pregnant girlfriend. The other he maintained was a sheriff, but he steadfastly refused to explain why the law would have an interest in his whereabouts.

As it turned out, Kenny had a cousin, a cousin who needed a job. And, as he explained to the Ranger in charge of our rag-tag crew, who better to take the extra bed on our floor?

I don't remember his cousin's name, but I do remember the long scar running from his hairline to his chin. Except for the cut, Kenny explained, his cousin was unhurt after he rocketed through a windshield. Being completely drunk, had, supposedly, erased his cousin's memory of the whole event.

Ken's cousin was a hard worker and quite affable, so he got on well with everyone. But his accident had not put him off having a few. Or many.

We were out in the bushes and a long way away from civilization which was Orofino, a tough little Idaho logging town. No one had a car so it was hard to go anywhere. But one Friday, Kenny's cousin somehow made it to town. When he came back late that night he was dead drunk, with a head full of mean. And he had a gun.

He was muttering as he staggered into the bunk house. I couldn't make out everything he said, but "kill all these fuckers" came through pretty clearly. He had a lever action rifle and a pocket full of bullets, many of which scattered over the floor as he flopped onto his bunk. He apparently had a lot of bullets though, and we could all hear the occasional round snicking home into the rifle's side loader as, still dropping bullets, he cursed in frustration.

While all this was going on, I saw Ervie select a work in progress cane with a huge burl on the end. In the middle of the bay was a big, old fashioned, wood burning stove. Miner Vic crept over and seized the handle of one of the stove's covers; damn thing must have weighed 10 pounds. Even Kenny snaked out a knife from somewhere, cousin or no cousin. For my part, I leaped from bed in my underwear. Looking back, I must have been planning to brain the guy with an apple from the label of my Fruit of the Looms. Other than that, I had nothing. I did get a nod from Ervie, however, as I joined the fray.

With mayhem about to commence, the sound of the lever action as a round was chambered and ready to fire, was really loud. At that moment, Kenny's cousin dropped the rifle.

He leaned over to pick it up, and over and over until he did a face plant. The next sound we heard was snoring. Kenny's cousin had passed out cold, laying on top of his loaded gun. None of us had touched him.

Kenny was up early the next morning to speak with the Ranger. A short time later a Forest Service truck pulled up. His cousin was given his gun and his bullets, which I thought was pretty stupid. He was then escorted to the truck and delivered...somewhere.

Ervie walked up to me. "Here," he said handing me a piece of metal.

I turned it over in my hand. "What's this?"

"A firing pin," he responded shaking his head at my stupidity.

The rifle had been rendered into a club by the simple removal of the firing pin. I still have it somewhere.

1. http://www.historyplace.com/speeches/joseph.htm

Chapter Three

"I'm lazy! I hate work! Hate hard work in all its forms! Clever shortcuts, that's all I'm about!" Eliezer Yudowsky

Forest Lesson Three was that if you're going to be a slacker, do it as part of a large group where it's not so noticeable. Barring that, don't shirk in a small group of guys used to hard, physical labor...try to pick instead a small bunch focused on knitting or proving the Earth is flat. If there's no escape, do the work and try to smile; the alternative is worse.

The Day We Humped A Cement Mixer Up The Mountain

The Ranger picked Vic to be foreman of the dreaded "Build A Dam On The Mountain" project.

Vic used more snus (a disgusting tobacco concoction) than was good for any six people, and mostly swallowed what he didn't spit. He said he picked up the habit in the Virginia Coal mines. We all quickly learned that when working with him being down wind was a really bad idea. Snus is the moist tobacco you can still buy in small, round tins. You gain its rather doubtful pleasures by sticking a wad of it between the inside of your cheek and your gum. I tried it one time and drunk or sober I will never try it again.

Vic was a really a hard-worker and a friend to those who followed suit. If he identified you as being O.K., you would be endlessly badgered to join him in a pilgrimage to the only whore house in Orofino, Idaho. Vic had a speech impediment. He couldn't pronounce "th" which came out "v" as in "bruvver." Not one of us ever had the stones to give him any crap about it.

I had hitch hiked from Minnesota to Idaho with Stu, a fraternity friend, to work for the summer in the firefighting arm of the Forest Service. Stu, already beer bellied at the age of 20, was in the same bunk house as Vic and I. Stu was moved out right after Vic stood nose to nose and quietly told him the next time he didn't do his share of the work, he'd get the snot beat out of him. Unfortunately, the lecture didn't stick.

A couple of days after Vic's one-sided chat with Stu, five of us, including Vic and Stu, got the short straw to build a small dam to provide the water needs of our line camp; a necessity as we were out in the middle of forest nowhere. This project required us to roll out before dawn and hike for some miles straight up the side of the mountain abutting the back of our camp. Once there, we were to build a small dam which would feed us the kind of sparkling mountain stream water which is now four bucks a bottle at Starbucks. Some other sorry bastards had already run pipe all the way up to the dam site, which truly must have been a terrible job. At least we didn't have to do that, we encouraged ourselves.

When we finally arrived close to the dam site, we found we then had to hump a helicopter deposited, 1900s vintage, one cylinder ("one lunger") cement mixer a half mile or so more, straight up to where we were to dam the stream. We then had to go back down to the drop site below for assorted bags of cement and cement block and hand haul it all up as well. Following that we were to dam the stream and get the water flowing; all to be completed in one long Idaho day. And Idaho can produce some really long, hot, sticky days.

Mostly what I remember was looking at the dirt and pushing on that damn cement mixer. Jesus, it was heavy; an old cast iron, crank started cement mixer. We were sweating like pigs, cursing our fate and unable to even swat at the swarms of No-See-Ums, tiny black bugs that bit and plagued us the whole way. The five of us were all pretty miserable, except for Stu who was at the back of the mixer waving at bugs with one hand and half-heartedly pushing with the other. I do have to say that prior to that stifling summer day I had never believed that you could actually feel a human being pulsing with fury. Take it from me, Vic was looking back at Stu and radiating a trembling anger so monumental it was an elemental force.

Shit, I thought, Vic's going to kill the guy.

When we made it to the little plateau where we were going to pour the cement, Vic didn't say a word. He just picked up the hand crank which had to be used to fire up that miserable cement mixer, walked over to Stu, and jammed the crank into his belly. "Now you listen to me, you little prick. You start that mixer, and if you say one word I will hit you so Goddamned hard it will kill you and every member of your family." And he said this very, very softly.

Now turning a crank may not seem like much payback for being a slacker, but for those of you lucky souls who have never had to start a one-cylinder engine with a hand crank—which is about 99.9% of everybody anymore—it is almost always a miserable job. They take forever to start, which means endless hand cranking, and worse yet are prone to fire and reverse themselves. Picture this: you are cranking the piston and flywheel to the right and cranking and cranking and cranking. Suddenly, the single cylinder fires but instead of the flywheel going to the right, the way you've been cranking, it decides to go in the other direction. If you hear a snapping sound at that second, the crank has just broken your finger. Or your wrist.

To his credit, it seemed that Stu had finally figured out that what he was now involved with was no looming schoolyard tussle. He carefully walked around Vic, slammed the crank onto the mixer and started in. It would not start and would not start and would not start. Within minutes, Stu was wringing wet. And he started to curse, so creatively that particularly good epithets actually elicited a cheer or two from the rest of us. Then a "chuff!" followed by a high-pitched scream. The mixer had fired. It didn't start, but sure enough the flywheel had reversed itself from the direction Stu was cranking. The crank tore itself out of Stu's hand and fell to the ground taking a goodly bit of skin from every one of Stu's knuckles along the way.

"Piece of shit!" Stu screamed. He grabbed the crank and threw it as hard as he could down the side of the mountain. In fairness, he did get some loft on it; in utter silence we all watched as the arc of the only thing that could start the cement mixer hit its apex and fell out of sight.

Stu weighed 300 pounds if he weighed an ounce, but Vic picked him up and shook him like a dog shakes a chew toy. I don't remember exactly the words that were said, but the totally one-sided berserker conversation began with our not being able to finish the job without the crank and moved on to spittle flecked shrieks regarding character traits and personal habits. It ended with Vic throwing Stu down the side of the mountain in the general direction of the now missing crank. Vic was a head shorter than Stu, but all rawhide and whipcord muscle from his work in the mines. He actually achieved both height and distance with his Stu toss while simultaneously shaking off the rest of us who were trying to stop him. I swear to God, I don't know why Stu didn't break his neck; he actually bounced multiple times before skidding to a stop. Vic then started chucking rocks at him screaming that he'd better find that crank, and if he tried to leave or came back up without it, no one would ever find his body.

It took Stu two hours, but he found the crank. And brought it back.

I took pity on him and started cranking the mixer myself, which luckily fired right up without kicking back. But there wasn't an ounce of pity in Vic. He handed Stu a shovel and worked right beside him during the rest of that long, sweltering day. Stu faltered once. Vic immediately hit him on the ass with the flat of his shovel. He hit him so hard he knocked Stu on his face and the flat "crack!" of the shovel actually produced an echo from the surrounding hills. "Get up," was all he said then, and handed Stu back his shovel.

We got it done, very late in the day but totally done. The cool, sweet water reached the camp long, long before we did. Though downhill, our descent was pretty slow. We were bone weary and Stu was limping badly, so we took it easy. Stu had not said one word since he returned the crank, nor did he speak as we trudged back to camp in the lengthening twilight. He angrily shook off our offers of help, so we left him alone to his silence and his limp and his thoughts.

Vic was bringing up the rear. I fell back alongside.

I was too damn tired to watch my tongue. "That was quite a...a... display today." Oops. I suddenly realized I probably didn't want to be poking a stick at the guy who had just thrown someone down a mountain.

Vic looked at me out of the corner of his eye. "You think so?"

"Well...yeah. I mean, you were pretty pissed and..." realizing I didn't know where I was going, I shut the hell up. We walked on in silence. Vic looked over at me. "There's nothing worse for a crew than a shirker. And there's nothing worse for a man than to dump his load on someone else."

I thought it over. "Well, Stu sure worked hard this afternoon."

This time the silence stretched on until we could see the lights of the camp. "My granddaddy worked the mines," Vic said suddenly. "Then my daddy, then my bruvver, then me. They taught me how to break a mule and they taught me how to make a man work."

What? I stopped. "And what of all that shit about 'no one will ever find the body?'"

Vic laughed out loud. "He brought back the crank, didn't he?"

We, all of us, finished out the summer. All of us, except Stu who caught a Greyhound Bus for home that Sunday.

CHAPTER FOUR

"Leadership is not a position or title, it is action and example." Cory Booker

"Because if there's one thing you want in a whorehouse, it's nice chairs." John Steinbeck, Of Mice and Men

Screw around in the woods long enough, and something unexpected—and usually bad—is going to happen. When it does, in the woods or anywhere else, a few folks react well, some badly; others just freeze in place. And you never know who is going to do what.

The experience of a close brush with death changes some people forever. In this case, it meant dragging team mates to a whorehouse, not surprisingly with bad result.

The Day We Went To Orofino

Our trip to Orofino really began when Vic was bleeding out on the mountain.

As mentioned in other Tales, with a buddy, I had hitched hiked to Idaho a couple of months previously for a summer of fighting fire. The summer's activity turned out to be mostly back-breaking grunt work in-between occasional, and terrifying, lightning -strike fires in the deep woods.

On this particular day, eight of us had been assigned to an old Suburban with bad, squealing brakes. Limping along, we were ferried up on immensely pot holed, old Forest Service roads almost to the top of one of the mountains in the Clearwater National Forest. Our assignment was to clear brush from and re-build some old hiking trails.

I had come to know all the members of our crew with one exception: A new guy, who had quickly acquired from us the moniker of Silent Ned. I mean, this guy just never said anything. Communication was limited to head nods and monosyllables of which we had identified four: "yes," "no," "what" and "here." This lead to a lot of speculation as to his background when he first arrived. The favorite guesses were raised by wolves, military, or ax-murderer. This speculation dribbled off fairly quickly. In our little rag-tag bunch no one really gave a damn. If you worked hard and didn't cause problems, you were in. Silent Ned kept totally to himself. Plus he worked really, really hard, so within a couple of weeks, he was totally accepted and everyone wanted Silent Ned on their crew.

We had each been issued a razor sharp, double bit ax and a shovel for the day's activities. I was clearing brush when I started hearing some incoherent screaming below, quite different in tone and tenor from our normal, grab-ass tomfoolery.

Vic, our crew chief, was an ex-coal miner with an explosive temper. He was prickly to deal with on occasion, but for some strange reason I had come to like him. I heard him shout once "I cut the artery in my arm!" He had been ax cutting branches and had notched his ax in a tree to keep it off the ground as he reached down for the branches. As bad luck would have it, at that moment, the ax fell and struck the inside of his upper arm. His brachial artery was severed instantly. The brachial artery is the major blood vessel of the upper arm. If it's cut, your odds of survival are about 35%...and that's if you get medical help in under 30 minutes; some say in less than 15 minutes.

By the time I had stumbled down the hillside to the van, Vic was laid out in the back seat. Blood was pulsing out of his arm. Another of our team, who had just started Paramedic training, had his fingers in the wound, trying to pinch off the blood flow. He was wild eyed and covered in blood. He was screaming "I can't stop it, I can't stop it!" Vic was ashen faced. "Help me fellows, help me" he kept saying weakly.

"Hold his arm, up, hold his arm up!" It was Silent Ned, silent no longer. He was literally running straight down the side of a really steep slope. "You!" he pointed to another of our crew when he slid to a stop "Take off your boot and give me the lace!"

"You!" he said to the budding Paramedic, "put pressure on that wound. Grip it as hard as you can!"

The boot lace and a stick made a quick tourniquet, but the blood just would not stop. Ah God, there was so much blood. Ned banged on the side of the van with his fist. "Quick! Who drove this piece of shit up here?" Another of our crew feebly raised his hand. "Well, get behind the wheel and fire it up; you're taking us back down!"

He leaned over Vic, whose eyes had started to flutter. Ned slapped him once, twice. "Stay with us, stay with us!"

Vic's eyes opened up. "You hit me again," he whispered, "and I'll rip your dick off."

Now Ned was on the radio. "Brush Crew to base, Brush Crew to base!"

"I thought I told you guys to stay off the radio," came Ranger Bob's laconic reply.

Ned was shouting now, into the radio. "We have a man down, I say again we have a man down! Bad arm wound. We've put a tourniquet on it, but we need a medivac or he's not going to make it! Call in the chopper; we'll meet it at the meadow on the south end!" Medivac? I thought. Chopper? What?

Ned threw himself into the Suburban's back seat with Vic. "Go, go, go, go, go!"

The van lurched away. We could hear the brakes screeching all the way down.

Silence fell. None of the rest of us, left behind, looked at each other. After a few minutes, the radio crackled to life. Ranger Bob was talking to someone, but we could only hear his side of the conversation.

"Thanks for sending the helicopter," said Ranger Bob. "One of our crew cut his arm and those idiots on the mountain put a tourniquet on it. I'm afraid he'll will lose his arm because of that if we don't get him to the hospital."

Now we looked at each other. Idiots on the mountain?

The next morning, Ranger Bob called us together. He started off by telling us that Vic would probably make it. He went on to say that he was told that when the helicopter Paramedics got their hands on him and started plasma, Vic only had minutes left. Then he said "I owe all of you an apology. I know you heard what I said on the radio, but the fact is you saved his life."

"Um, actually," said the guy who drove the Suburban down to meet the helicopter, "We didn't save Vic's life." He pointed to Ned, now silent again. "He did."

As we all murmured our agreement, Ned didn't say a word. He just turned and walked out of the Ranger's office. We heard his car driving away moments later. Silent Ned never came back.

Vic, however, did come back just a couple of weeks later. Stitches, over a hundred, were now out. Vic would proudly show off his puckered, still healing wound at the slightest provocation. Without let up he used his near-death experience as the reason we should all take a Friday night excursion together to Orofino, Idaho. After refusing to join him in such expeditions all summer, we now decided to honor his request and go. Without Silent Ned, there were seven of us in our crew, one of whom had a car. The road trip would be a tight squeeze in a single car, but Orofino was less than an hour away.

The gold around the town of Orofino (Spanish for "fine gold") had played out before the 1900's. When I was there, it had become a loggers' town of under 3,000 souls, its population and trouble swelling greatly on Friday and Saturday nights.

With Vic acting as tour guide we were unerringly directed to a two-story building on the edge of town. The bottom floor was a bar. The second, Vic proudly explained, housed the only whorehouse in Orofino.

Only one other of us decided to join Vic in an excursion upstairs; the rest of our little band, myself included, decided the grungy little bar offered enough distraction for a Friday night.

We weren't the only customers. There were probably a dozen or so rough looking dudes there as well, undoubtedly loggers in town for a little R&R. They were gathered at one end of the bar. Another couple of tables by the door were filled with a handful of Forest Service guys like us which was actually a bit surprising.

We all minded our own business...except a loud, younger guy at one of the tables filled with fellow Forest Service workers. The guy was pretty drunk and really had a mouth on him. His friends tried to quiet him down, but he just would not shut up. He was loudly talking about what a shit bar we were all in and went on to make other observations not very complimentary if you happened to actually like the bar or lived in Orofino. The Loudmouth got up making one last comment about leaving so the other patrons would be free to sexually molest forest animals unobserved.

That apparently was just too much.

A bullet-headed, logger-type at the bar shook his head and walked over to the Loudmouth. He grabbed his arm, spun him around and hit him so damn hard the Loudmouth was actually lifted off the floor. This was something I had only read about, but never seen. It's something I hope to never see again.

My own fisticuff experience had ended when I was about twelve. My bar fighting experience was zero. I don't know what, if anything, I intended to do when I stepped towards the Loudmouth, now obviously out cold on the floor. Instantly someone grabbed the center of my shirt in a bunched fist, and I found myself up against the bar. The guy holding me brought his other hand up from below the bar smashing a bottle against the bar's edge as he did so. He pressed the jagged edge to my cheek, just below my right eye and said "Don't."

I didn't and was forced to stand still and watch a terrible scene unfold. I honestly had thought the fight, such as it was, was over. The Loudmouth was down for the count so my school yard experience told me everyone would just stop now. The bullet-headed man didn't stop; he started kicking the guy on the floor in the face with his big work boots. He kicked him over and over until the bartender started shouting, "Joe, take it outside!"

Joe took it outside through the simple expedient of throwing the Loudmouth through the door and onto the street.

The guy holding me said, "Kid, get outta here," and threw me towards the door as well. I was glad to go.

By the time we all got outside, Joe the bullet-headed guy was astride the Loudmouth, repeatedly smashing him in the face with his fists. Two of Orofino's finest had shown up. One of them had uncertainly pulled his gun. The other, obviously knew the hitter. "Joe!" he was shouting, pulling at him. "Joe, stop! You'll kill him! Joe, stop it!"

The pummeling slowed and stopped. "Fred?" said the hitter looking up. "Yeah," the cop replied. "Joe, what's the matter with you?" Joe looked down as his very beaten and bloody opponent. "I didn't like what he said."

I turned around to find Vic and his fellow second floor visitor standing in the bar's doorway. They looked at the crowd and the flashing lights of the police car. Vic cocked his head at the warble of an approaching siren, clearly not an unfamiliar sound. It was an ambulance as it turned out.

He started laughing. "You should have gone upstairs with us."

The rest of the summer passed without further incident.

The day I left Idaho, as I was waiting outside for my ride to the bus station, Ervie walked out onto the bunkhouse steps. Why I don't know, but Ervie hated us college guys. Deeply. "College shitheads" was his mildest adjective. The oldest of our motely gang, he had worked in the woods for many, many years. His bad road face showed every day of it.

"Hey, Shithead," he called out to me. "You did all right."

"Gee, Ervie, thanks. I thought…"

"Ah, go fuck yourself," he muttered as he walked back inside.

It never occurred to me that my bag was unduly heavy as I lugged it a couple thousand miles back home. Once there, I found at the bottom of my duffle a big river rock signed, in most cases rudely, by my weird, Idaho friends.

As the years have passed, I've received my share of compliments and an occasional award. But in truth none have meant so much to me as that river rock and the comment "Hey, Shithead, you did all right."

CHAPTER FIVE

"Any self-respecting entrepreneur has borrowed money from their mother at some point." Kevin Plank

Enough of Life Lessons from the woods already. Here's one about working: Having initial entrepreneurial success ruins you forever for a regular job.

The Day We Sparked A Riot In Fargo North Dakota

When I was introduced to the manager of Paul Revere and the Raiders, he didn't even shake my hand. He just stared fixedly through the curtains at the boiling crowd. "Jesus Christ," he kept saying, "Jesus Christ! Where the hell are we? Fargo? Fargo! Jesus Christ!"

A buddy of mine and I had launched a Concert agency in lieu of studying. My contributions to the partnership were the proceeds from selling my bike (no, not THAT kind of bike; a Schwinn. Red. Pedals. Balloon tires) and access to my father's hi-fi speakers, normally used to provide music to his Square Dance club.

Paul Revere and the Raiders, who have receded into the mists of time, were a huge band back then when they were booked into Fargo by we lads from Moorhead Minnesota, a small town right across the river from Fargo, North Dakota. The band sported ersatz, colonial costumes, boasted national hits, and the lead singer almost got electrocuted on the stage during our show...which we later found out was a shtick.

Our prior Rock events, such as they were, were held at the Moorhead Armory in Moorhead, Minnesota. This venue had achieved fame for being the site of "The Day The Music Died." Buddy Holly, the Big Bopper, and Richie Valens were killed together in an airplane crash in a wintery Iowa cornfield as they flew to a concert at the Armory.

This tragic event launched the career of a 15-year-old Fargo kid, who filled in. His name was Bobby Vee. My mother subsequently managed his fan club from her record store in downtown Fargo. He went on to become a teen heart throb and sang the lead on many national, hit records. His career was ultimately tanked by the arrival of the Beatles and the rest of the 60's "British Invasion").

We had no damn business booking a national act but book them we did.

And here's what happened:

Our "agency" was in full swing. My buddy and I were making what to us at the time were gobs of money, and happily squandering it all. I still sweat thinking of it today, and sadly wish we'd paid more attention to the term "compound interest."

Somehow my partner got word that Paul Revere and the Raiders were going to do a gig in Minneapolis, which is almost Fargo/Moorhead if you squinch your eyes when looking at a GPS. We called their manager; I still remember the pitch: "Just stop in Fargo on your way to Minneapolis. Play one session, get back on the plane carrying a box of money!"

I later asked their manager why he took us up on it. "I was drunk," he replied.

They nailed us for, like, 40% of the gross. I don't think they could have gotten more with a gun. When the band hit the Fargo Auditorium, there must have been 10,000 screaming kids in the place; we had emptied every farm for miles around. Fire marshals were threatening lock down. DJs were hysterically egging on more folks to come to the concert. Our buddies were letting people in the side doors for cash.

I don't remember much about the concert except for the screaming and my prayers that no one would be pushed through the glass doors...that and the electrocution thing, which looks pretty corny in retrospect but sure drew a gasp from the crowd. The "electrocution" consisted of the lead singer fiddling with the plug wire to his guitar. Then came a loud, buzzing noise. This was immediately followed by a twitching, St. Vitus type dance which concluded with the lead singer falling to the floor. As the crowd began shouting in dismay, other band members ran over to their fallen comrade. Resuscitation, miracle-like in its brevity, came to pass immediately.

Then, it was over and we really did have a box full of money. A cardboard box. A BIG cardboard box. No credit cards. No advance ticket sales and no checks, just cold, hard cash.

"Well," says I, "probably we should go down to the police station to count this. It's late and this is a lot of money, and...and..." I dribbled to a stop as the Manager gave me the fish eye, unwrapped a cigar and slowly puffed it to life. "Now son," says he, "the police, those fine folks, have enough to do already. There must be somewhere else we can do the count, somewhere...quiet. Informal. Can't have my lads being badgered for autographs."

Silence fell.

My partner broke in. "How about my parents' place?" he offered.

Cut to his parents' kitchen table, 1:00 AM. Everyone is gathered around a mound of money, intent like Dobermans looking at a chicken leg.

The count was carefully done. "One for us, two for you, one for us, two for you..." As we split the money up, the Manager took his cut from the Raiders' pile, and then each of the five Raiders took their share from the remainder. To make sure all of the proceeds were properly reported, the Manager and his Raider team stuffed the money in their pockets, undoubtedly putting the Social Security withholding tax in the front left pocket; income tax due into the back right. For our part, we dropped our take back into the cardboard box, a well-known accounting procedure.

When we were done, the Raiders trooped out. Their Manager lingered for a final, and now fond farewell. He mouth-rolled his cigar from left to right and shook our hands. "Thanks, boys. Call me any time." And off he went with one final mutter: "Fargo, Jesus Christ!"

CHAPTER SIX

"Drink heavily with locals whenever possible" Anthony Bourdain

Here's a couple of Life Lessons gleaned from travel. The first, which is probably good to take to heart, is that drinking heavily with locals often leads to getting involved with shit you'd never do otherwise.

The Day We Went Shark Fishing In Our Underwear

The three of us were standing in waist deep surf. In our underwear. In the dead of night. Shark fishing.

I remember thinking "this is probably a really bad idea" and no, we weren't drunk. The big, greasy hunk of raw meat on the end of a huge hook, tethered to a rope-like line I was gripping tightly, just had to be spreading blood in the water.

It was a beautiful night though, there on the north side of Trinidad on my last day on the island. We had earlier motored to Jim's Grandmother's place outside of Toco to give her a hand in cleaning up her house. Her much lived in home was still located by a fallow cocoa plantation, owned generationally by Jim's family for as long as anyone could remember. The house was a huge place, with just her rattling around inside of it. While currently in disrepair, the tropical home clearly at one time had been the center of a large family and many glittering events. It now sported out of control foliage, peeling paint, rickety stairs and a lot of webs spun by huge jungle arachnids of indeterminate origin and intent.

We cleansed the house of both spider and web, ruining a number of brooms in the process, and adjourned in victory to a local bar with dirt floor décor and one chuffing refrigerator, which meant cold beer. The joint was packed.

By my second beer, Jim had disappeared. A man walked up and begin talking. Loudly. Angrily.

"Why me," I thought then realized that picking me out of the bar crowd would have been only marginally harder had I been a pig wearing britches.

I smiled and tried to be pleasant, but the loudness from my new friend turned to shouting and gestures. The problem with my "be pleasant" plan was that I couldn't understand a damn word he said, he shouting in island patois and I having nothing to draw on but American slang.

Then he pulled a knife.

I remember it as being a big, big knife...but it probably really wasn't all that large. Because what he pulled and deployed was a "snap knife." That's the kind of knife, much favored back then by workers in the tropics, which conceals a wicked blade until the wielder palms it and "snaps" their wrist. Upon that movement, the blade instantly pops out and locks in place, ready for whatever business is at hand.

Unfortunately, at that moment I appeared to be the business at hand. And I can personally testify that in such situations, the room temperature actually does drop by about 6 degrees.

As I frantically cast about for an escape route, Jim appeared with his arm around the shoulders of another guy, obviously a friend (It turned out to be his uncle). They broke through the circle of onlookers, who I believe were placing bets, and started laughing at my knife wielding acquaintance. This was a tactic I had not thought to employ, but fortunately for me it did the trick since the knife guy was an old school chum of my host, Jim.

Mr. Knife then bought me a beer, under the basic heading of "no hard feelings, eh?" I couldn't understand that either, of course, but I figured on top of all of my other troubles there must be an earthquake going on as the free bottle of beer was shaking badly as I raised it to my lips.

Jim's uncle watched this in silence. Without resorting to patois he said "You need to come shark fishing with me and Jim. Tonight."

I had arrived in Trinidad some days earlier, as an invited guest of my college chum Jim, a native Trinidadian and member of Trinidad's Olympic team. He was a runner, and although he didn't medal, he was FAST. At his invitation, I raced him on the water buffalo infested training track he had frequented for years in order to gain a slot on the team. Not being into continual humiliation, I only did that once.

Jim went out of his way to introduce me to various aspects of Island culture. I was particularly enthralled with three things: a lethal concoction of rum and fruit juice that was poured into a machete-opened green coconut full of its milk; second, steel drum bands which seemed to be everywhere, and third, a delicious Trinidadian snack called a Roti, a sort of spicy burrito stuffed with meat.

Prior to our expedition to Grammas house, we had hung out exclusively in Port of Spain on the other side of the island. Interesting place that and still a cruise line destination, I understand, as ships can pull up, dock, and be virtually downtown thereby spilling tourists directly out into the city and into the loving arms of various hustlers. Although I understand things are vastly tamer now, back then it was all still a bit wild, albeit beautiful. We were sitting in an outdoor café overlooking the ocean when a cruise ship appeared on the horizon.

Jim looked at me over the edge of his glass. "Watch this," he said, pointing out the steel band that magically appeared placing itself right in the path of the tourists being disgorged out onto the dock. Almost all the tourists appearing were older and couples, so there wasn't much for the prostitutes to do in one sense, but most of them were dual career as they were also accomplished pickpockets and ad hoc members of the band.

I never would've noticed the hustle had it not been for Jim pointing it all out. The beautiful music of the steel band brought everyone to a halt, cameras snapping. The pickpocket, auxiliary members of the band flowed smoothly through the crowd, lightening the pockets of God knows how many of the ship's passengers. Then all of them faded away just as the first anguished cries of "Hey, my wallet!" began to drift up from the dock.

We adjourned to my favorite Roti stand for a cheap bite of lunch. I had a favorite Roti dish with a side of rice. I don't remember now what it was called but the Roti was filled with meat, the whole dripping bundle seeming quite delicious and exotic.

Just before I left the island, my favorite Roti stand, along with numerous others owned by the same person, was shuttered and torn down in a lightning raid by the authorities. It seems that no one cared much when the stray dogs had started to disappear. But when the rat population virtually evaporated, the local authorities added the missing dogs and the missing rats together in a sort of 1+1 equals "this is disgusting" formula and took action. I was told later that it took some weeks, but gradually the stray dog and rat population returned to what was considered normal for the area.

So now my last day on the island had arrived, punctuated with dead spiders and a derailed bar fight.

Jim and his Uncle extracted me from the bar without further incident and we went over to the Uncle's house. Once darkness fell, we traipsed through what seemed to me to be dense jungle. After a considerable time, we arrived at the beach, where I now found myself pantless and waist deep in shark infested, tropical waters holding a line attached to a hunk of raw meat. We had all removed our pants and shoes because, as Jim's uncle put it, "we don't want to walk back in wet clothes." It wasn't until we were in the water that it occurred to me that perhaps all that bare skin now just made us look tastier.

Since nothing was happening, strangely enough it was actually peaceful standing in the moonlight dappled water. Right up until something, a big something, hit the Uncle's line.

He started skidding out to sea. We grabbed him, and the line, and soon the three of us pulled a very large ocean dweller with big snapping teeth up onto the beach. It wasn't a shark. I don't know what it was, and probably never will know. It was about 6 feet long, and thicker than the biggest anaconda anyone has ever lied about; an eel of some sort. I seem to remember it was hissing as well as enthusiastically gnashing a mouth full of very sharp teeth. But I have been told on the best authority that sea creatures don't hiss, so surely I must be mistaken.

Jim's uncle cheerfully picked up a big rock and beat the sea creature about the head and its nonexistent shoulders until calmness prevailed. He then announced that fishing was over and we pulled our lines in. My huge piece of bait was totally gone and I hadn't felt a thing.

It seemed like we walked forever through the dark foliage carrying that damn whatever it was before we arrived back at the house. Once there I was invited in for something to eat; a delightful prospect which I gratefully and immediately accepted.

Inside, Jim's Uncle slapped our catch down onto the kitchen table. Producing a hammer, he then nailed the head securely onto the one of the table's planks. He cut a "T" behind the head and just a bit down the backbone separating the skin, which I remember as being bright yellow, dappled with brown spots. In a single motion, with the help of a pliers, the skin was pulled off like a sticky sock.

So we capped off the day with fried Denizen Of The Deep filet, supping on the table alongside the carcass of the creature that had given its all for our meal. I remember the entree as being delicious. And it didn't taste a bit like chicken.

CHAPTER SEVEN

"There comes a time in the affairs of man when he must take the bull by the tail and face the situation". W.C. Fields.

"'The probability of someone laughing at you is proportional to the stupidity of your actions" Author Unknown

The second Travel Life Lesson is: don't go somewhere and do something you inherently know is stupid just because it takes place in a different locale.

The Day I Ran with the Bulls

Today, a million and a half tourists absolutely pack Pamplona for the bull running fiesta. ESPN covers the event live, and it's all quite comparatively organized. The town now has a population of over 200,000 up from a sleepy 30,000 not so long ago. The Spanish kids by and large now stay away from what used to be considered another of those stupid rites of passage for young men.

When I was in Pamplona, so long ago now, were things better, "more real?" Nope. Only those with really bad memories or those living in a fantasy world would think so. But I grant you, it was really different.

So after Hemmingway, post lost generation but pre-flowerchild, before ESPN, before Go-Pro, before worldwide, live TV coverage and almost two million tourists yearly, here's how it was to run with the bulls in Pamplona.

The Norwegian damn near knocked me out when he threw me into a doorway. Trying to keep me from getting hurt, he left himself wide open. A bull then slammed square into his chest.

The last I saw of him until the run was over was him bouncing down the street with both arms wrapped around the horns on either side of a bull's head. He was easily thrown off and then the animal ran right over him.

The decision to journey to Pamplona was in fact a product of having no other immediate plans and being extraordinarily hung over. The prospect of recovering from a Paris birthday party on a train going...somewhere...was much more of a determining factor than any Hemmingway inspired vision from The Sun Also Rises. In fact, I didn't even read his damn book until years later. Now, I'm told that a journey to the bull fiesta in Pamplona requires a lot of advance planning and reservations. Then, we just got on the train. Plenty of seats.

By the time my travel buddy, Bruce, and I reached Pamplona, I'm surprised we weren't dead from salmonella. Rattling and rickety old trains took us across Spain. We moved slowly enough that leaning out the windows to buy egg sandwiches from any of countless vendors, worked on the entire Paris to Pamplona railway run. I remember the dripping sandwiches as being wrapped in dirty paper and delicious. Each sandwich undoubtedly carried sufficient lurking bacteria to lay low every health inspector on the planet today, but amazingly we never got sick. Well, not too sick anyway.

We had, of course, no place to stay in Pamplona. Which was O.K. because we were too broke to pay for lodging. We ended up in a park, gone now I understand, which was festooned with tents and the sleeping bags of other pilgrims too broke—or cheap—to pay for hotel rooms. We had a couple of cloth suitcases, but no tent, no sleeping bag, no blankets.

"You American?" A beer bellied guy with a young boy in tow (his son as it turned out), looked us up and down. A Spanish teacher from Michigan, he subsequently took pity and produced a couple of spare blankets and an offer for us to bed down next to his tent.

"Shitter is over there," he thumb pointed to a low, stone building. His timing was good since, as it turned out, we were both getting some egg sandwich backup.

Now, as a kid I spent summers on farms with no running water and no indoor plumbing. So privies were not a mystery or abhorrent to me. But in that Pamplona park I was introduced for the first time to the "squat over a hole in the floor" toilet. Plus, the men's section was attended by three or four middle aged ladies. But no big deal. What turned out to be a big deal was when, as soon as my pants were down around my ankles, the door was whipped open followed by a broken-English pitch from one of the ladies to buy some toilet paper. I will say that getting some money out of my pants to make a purchase proved to be difficult and embarrassing.

When I emerged, my travel buddy was sitting on our donated blankets cursing the toilet paper scam, which honestly, I found to be pretty funny.

He cursed some more. "I didn't buy any of their damn paper," he shouted. That, I thought, was quite extraordinary. "So, what did you do?" I asked.

He glared at me. "I used my handkerchief. And then I threw it down the hole." I never asked him, nor did I wish to discover, what he did from that point on.

We had arrived on the second day of the Fiesta, the Festival of San Fermin, the day folks actually start running with the bulls every morning (the first day was spent, and still is, I understand, basically spraying wine on everyone around you). There seems to be some argument as to whether the Saint actually existed, but there's no argument that records show the festival dates back to at least the 13th century.

The goal we soon found out was to drink all night, run with the bulls in the morning, and then sleep the day away. Repeat for eight days. We were more than fine with all the elements of the Fiesta, except for the bulls part.

The all night, ever rolling party in the town square was something I had never seen...or imagined. Thousands of people. Fights all over. Everyone drunk and shouting. Kids running at top speed through the roiling crowd, pushing wheelbarrows with bulls' horns on the front and full of blazing fireworks. After a few days, bandages began to appear as revelers got banged up from partying alone, never mind running with any bulls.

We tapped our dwindling funds to buy a couple of botas (wineskins). What we didn't know is that the cheap wineskins, which is what we bought of course, were wine-proofed with a kind of fish-oil tar. It was highly recommended that such wineskins be "cured" for few days by filling them with cheap wine, which was then to be poured out and replaced. We cured our botas for about two minutes, pouring the wine into ourselves. It tasted awful, but we drank it anyway, noticing the wine seemed to get better as the days went by.

In truth, if I hadn't tripped over the Norwegian, I never would have run with the bulls.

It was just getting light. We'd been up all night and I was weaving through the campground trying to find our humble nest of borrowed blankets. I was almost there when I stumbled over a guy wrapped around a really big wineskin. I think he was snoring gently until I stepped on his head.

"Let's have a drink!" he shouted in passable English after he ascertained I was a rather harmless looking American hoping not to get punched. "Let's have a drink! Then we run!"

He introduced himself and at some point allowed as how he was a member of the Norwegian *Hærens Fallskjermjegerskole*, which I came to discover was the equivalent of Norway's special forces (It's now called Hærens Jegerskolethe).

"I run here every year...stay sharp! You run with me, yes? I watch out for you!"

We started in on his wine. When we were almost finished: "You run with me, yes?"

"Sure," I answered.

It was now almost 8:00 AM and time for the day's run to start. Being a runner then had only a few loose rules: first, be male (that restriction is now gone); second, be over 18 and third, be sober. We were rock solid on two of the three.

It's said that bull runs, such as the one in Pamplona, began when bulls needed to be moved from their corrals to the bull ring for later bull fights. The bulls were just herded down the streets. Then, young lads full of the macho spirit started running with the bulls in a little *mano a cow*. This morphed into a fiesta. Since record keeping started in 1910, 15 people have been killed in Pamplona runs. From what I read, while there's a lot of injuries and gorings now, no one has been killed since 2012. These days, 16 medical stations, manned in total by 200 people, are set up every 40 feet or so with 20+ ambulances standing by. I don't recall anything of the sort when I was there, but then fear tends to wipe the peripheral memory.

We were wandering along the bull run when I heard a loud bang. That was the rocket going off which announced that the corral gate was open and 12 big, grumpy animals were on the loose. Six of these, wicked horns intact, were bulls destined for the ring that afternoon. Six were heifers, but damn big bovine ladies, also sporting huge horns. The heifers wore bells to alert the runners that trouble was on the way, but as bulls and cows alike could all run the entire distance at 35 MPH, the warning of the bells was generally moot.

My Norse guide shouted something in Norwegian and began to run, pulling me along by the arm. It only took a short distance for it to be clear that we were running in the wrong direction; towards the bulls, not away. I later learned that the real whack jobs would start their run by racing towards the bulls as they were released.

Suddenly the crowd scrambled aside and we saw a number of bulls headed in our direction. In danger, it is conventional wisdom that normal human beings immediately take one of two options, fight or flight. Well, there's a third option called "stupidly freeze in place," which I immediately utilized. It was at this juncture that my crazy friend paused his own escape to throw me out of mid-street into a narrow doorway. And that's when he got nailed and disappeared from sight.

What I remember most was the screaming. Everyone was screaming, those watching and those running. And when the bulls would hit someone, the high-pitched crowd noise literally hurt the ears. The street was so packed that the only time you'd see a bull was when they were right on top of you, which is exactly what you did not want. The flight option kicked in; my little voice started shouting at me to get the hell out of there.

I ran off, at least in the right direction this time which was towards the bull ring where everyone, humans and animals, were headed. After being knocked down a couple of times by other runners, I noticed that side streets leading off the run were fenced off, but in such a way that a person could roll under or scale the boards and get off the street. Then I noticed something else. Those who tried to scale the fences were dropping back onto the street.

These days I read that the side streets are still fenced, but with a double fence. Spectators can only stand behind the second fence. Behind the first fence are medical and security folks who assist those hurt or who just want to abandon the run.

I never saw a double fence. What I did see was that those who leaped onto a fence to get out or out of the way were smashed in the face by guys shouting "Querías correr? Corre!" ("you wanted to run? Run!"). It quickly became apparent that those getting face punched were all easily identified as tourists. Like me.

So I kept going. The goal of each day's run is to get the bulls for that day's afternoon bull fights into the arena and into holding pens there. That means that not only do the bulls have to run into the ring, but they then have to be chased into holding pens. By the runners. I didn't know any of this at the time, but I really, truly did not want to be caught in the long, narrow concrete tunnel leading from the street into the bull ring. I figured that if you got hit there it would be horrific, pushed back against concrete walls and savaged. Later I was told that goring in the tunnel was not the problem. Rather, the problem was called a "montón," a runner pile up in the tunnel and subsequent asphyxia.

When I emerged from the tunnel into the bull ring, I did my second "freeze in place" of the day. The bull ring was packed to the rafters; 20,000 people, all also screaming at the top of their lungs.

There was a group of traditionally dressed men (white shirt and pants, red sash and red bandana) sitting on the sand in front of the tunnel. They had linked arms and were singing, which I thought at the time was pretty neat local color. One of them pulled me down on the sand to join the group. Seconds later I found out that this was another bunch of crazies who had some sort of club for the bravest of the brave who showed off by sitting right in front of where the by now really pissed off bulls ran into the arena.

As soon as the first bull shot out of the tunnel and smashed into the singers on the sand next to me, I leaped up, just in time to be nailed in the short ribs. Fortunately, I think it was by one of the heifers, as I remember the cheerful sound of bells and I didn't get actually gored. I did get thrown in the air however to the raucous laughter of the sand singers.

Soon enough, the bulls had all been chased into pens. A couple of runners had gotten hurt in the process, one of them pretty seriously gored. Other runners literally grabbed the huge bull as the goring began (and yes, some grabbed it by the tail) until it ran away from its victim, who was passed over the bull ring's wall, bleeding heavily.

The bull ring doors were thrown open so we could get out ourselves. The singers on the sand, who had gotten me cow thumped, thought it was all quite hilarious. They gestured for me to come along for, as it turned out, a morning of yet more drinking and food at some decrepit bar; their treat. As we emerged from the bull ring, there was the Norwegian.

He was sitting on the curb morosely staring at his bloody foot. The bull that had hit him in the chest, had stepped repeatedly on his feet, one of which was now missing three toe nails.

It must have hurt like hell, but he just shrugged and said, "Was fun, yes?"

When I got back to the campground, my travel buddy, Bruce,

wandered over. He was pretty dinged up.

"So, did you run too?"

He looked at me. "Are you nuts?" He went on to relate that he had met a lady who took him to an apartment overlooking the street. He spent, he said, the morning watching the dolts running with the bulls from a nice balcony.

He said all was going well until two guys stormed into the apartment shouting something which used the word "hermanos" (brothers) a lot.

Bruce gazed out over the park. "They threw me down the stairs."

I didn't say anything until he added "It could have been worse."

"How," I asked, "could it possibly have been worse?"

"At first, they were going to throw me over the balcony."

These days, the moral arc is bending in the right direction. Bullfights are going away in Spain, and may one day end everywhere forever, and good riddance. Now, two days before the running of the bulls in Pamplona, there's the animal activists' Running Of The Nudes along the same route. That's becoming almost as popular as the bull running. In New Orleans, the Big Easy Rollergirls, dressed as bulls, skate through the French Quarter after runners. The Starboard Bar in Dewey Beach Delaware hosts a yearly "Running of The Bull" consisting of two people in a cow suit chasing folks on the beach.

But the attraction of people to those who sneer at danger may keep things going for a while. Some years ago, I showed my then 16-year-old niece a clip of people running with the bulls. She watched in silence.

"What do you think?" I asked.

She looked up. "That's the stupidest thing I ever saw. What kind of an idiot would do that?"

Chapter Eight

"If you cannot get rid of the family skeleton, you may as well make it dance" G.B. Shaw

I've noticed that bragging about ancestors tends to be loudest about those most removed from present day. The further away in time relatives are, the more we tend to sanitize what they did...and forget that for most of them, life really sucked. Think chamber pot. I did know my Grandfather personally, though....

The Day the Game Warden Died

My Granddad shot Blackie under the big old tree in the center of the barnyard. My cousin Janet was lounging on a low branch, Alice in Wonderland style, with me down below. I don't remember what kid stuff my cousin and I were discussing, but I do remember my Granddad ordering Blackie, a mostly Labrador laying by my side, to go get the cows. He gave the "get the cows" order twice, and Blackie just cocked his head in that tongue lolling, brown-eyed way that Labradors have, and looked at him, clearly perplexed.

Grandad sighed, walked to the house, retrieved his worn, much used shotgun and killed Blackie right then and there, the crack of the gun twice punctuating my cousin's hysterical screaming. Then, without ceremony, he fired up his rickety tractor, pulled Blackie to the manure pile and dumped him up on top. Until she died many years later, Janet and I when together would occasionally bring up that day. But never for too long because she would start to cry and my eyeballs would start to sweat so we always changed the subject.

My Grandfather always wanted to be a veterinarian, but after sixth grade, more schooling was utterly impossible.

He had that touch, that magic that would calm an animal no matter how hurt or sick, bringing them rest and healing. No one bothered with farm dogs or barn cats back then; they lived, they died. If they weren't "useful", they were gotten rid of...there really were no pets. So neighbors would deliver to my Grandfather only their wounded and ill cash livestock for a last chance... and often it worked, thanks to my Grandfather's caring and gentle hands. But none of that really mattered; my grandparents were born just in time to be adults in the depression of the 1930s, that glacier of poverty and despair that either ground people to dust or turned them into rocks, hard and cold as ice.

My Granddad had a lot of dogs over the years and the ones that survived were great at bringing in the cows. How they came to know how to do this is an enduring mystery, as he never gave them a lick of training. He would just shout at them to do whatever he wanted them to do, expecting the dog in question to know what he was talking about and to follow orders. To my Grandmother's ongoing disgust and irritation, Granddad was the same with chickens—at night he would shout at them to go into the coop and then kill the ones that didn't follow orders. Time after time, in the early evening he would off handedly dump a half dozen or so dead chickens into the kitchen sink, which had no running water, and expect Grandmother to gut, pluck and prepare the chicken for cooking...before morning. And then he'd go to bed.

When I start to judge them, I try to remind myself that my Grandparents grew up in a different time, a time so different it might as well have been lived on another planet. "Having to get married," they had and raised six kids, two of them delivered by my Grandfather on the kitchen table.

That shiny old shotgun that killed Blackie saw service three other times that I know of. Once was when my Grandmother shot at a couple dozen of Grandad's relatives in order to drive them off their farm during the depression of the 1930's. She had stood by day after day as his relatives camped out in the apple orchard and ran up grocery bills that my Grandparents would have to pay...but then she found out one of them, who was hot bunking with her kids, had syphilis. She yanked that old gun out of the closet and marched out to the orchard. She banged away at them, fortunately clipping only the apple trees. By the time Granddad got home that evening, all the relatives were gone. They never came back.

Another time, gun in hand, my Grandfather faced down three New Deal agents who had come to his farm to kill his pigs under a government program designed to drive up livestock prices. But Granddad had six kids and his hogs weren't low priced, unsellable pigs, they were food. So he threatened to kill those Federal agents with that old shotgun. The agents left. The pigs survived to offer up many a ham sandwich and why Granddad didn't go to jail for what he did that day is still a family mystery.

The third, other time was one when I personally saw him use that gun, probably saving my life as a kid. Another cousin of mine (I have a lot of them) and I wandered down from the back porch into the barnyard at which point a huge full-grown bull, my Grandfather's pride and joy, came bursting out of the barn and directly towards us. I remember it had stopped to paw the ground directly in front of my cousin and I, a really bad sign, when my Granddad ran from the house towards us, shotgun in hand. My Grandfather loved that bull. He needed that bull. It was the only bull he had, and the calves he so desperately required to make ends meet were the progeny of that one fecund animal and my Grandparents' scraggly herd of heifers. Granddad started shooting that bull before he skidded to a halt beside us, and he shot it and he shot it and he shot it until that huge animal turned away bellowing and ran off, taking out part of the fence. I heard later that my grandfather was in such a rush he might've been shooting the bull with bird shot, not having had time to load buckshot. I don't know if the bull survived as I never saw it again. Either it died or my grandfather subsequently penned it up far away from the house.

In the 1930s, it got really bad for my Grandparents and their kids. The dust bowl was raging, even hitting parts of South Dakota where they lived. Drought. The crops failed. My Grandparents had moved to a farm bordering a lake and my Grandfather became famous as a guy who would catch fish out of that lake when no one else could even get a nibble. Those fish, one of my uncles later told me, saved the family. My uncle then added he could not stand the taste or smell of fish ever after, as that as was pretty much all they ate for a period of some years. There were limits on the number of fish you could catch and take home even then, so naturally my Grandfather poached.

One of my Granddad's best friends from childhood became the Game Warden for the entire county in which my Grandparents lived. Times were tough and the Game Warden's pay, I have no doubt, took care of and saved the Warden's family. Certainly, he could not afford lose that job, friend or no.

They became bitter enemies, the Game Warden and my Grandfather. Their enmity raged for years, so hostile and fierce that at times folks were afraid it would lead to killing violence.

The Game Warden, and everyone else, knew that my grandfather was poaching, and probably not just fish. Nailing my Grandfather became an ongoing "I'm doing my job" goal and constant "have you arrested him yet?" irritant for the Warden. Under this incessant goading, the Game Warden apparently one day decided that catching someone poaching fish was probably the easiest way to nail a miscreant, particularly in the winter when everyone used fish houses out on the ice.

The Game Warden took to showing up at my grandfather's fish house day and night, appearing out of the snow like some vengeful wraith, banging on the door and actually shouting "open in the name of the law!" He also would come by the farm, ongoing warrant in hand, looking for an excess of fish heads and entrails, but what with the always hungry sty of pigs on the premises never had any luck. Grandmother would offer him coffee.

I don't know if it ever became a game, but I do know my grandfather worked out an entire process and enlisted his kids, whenever he dragged them along to help out with the fishing. They would always throw a few fish outside of the fish house to freeze, making sure they were visible. They made sure all of the frozen fish met the size limit and that the number thrown outside was always fewer than the catching limit so it couldn't be argued that Granddad and the occupants of the fish house could not go on trying to snag yet more fish in order to hit the legal limit. It's a good thing that my Grandfather built a false wall into the fish house with just enough room between it and the real wall to slither in a lot of catch, as my Grandfather and now and again his kids caught a lot of fish, day and night.

The Game Warden never figured it out. Or rather having a family of his own to support and knowing the heart-stopping terror of it all, he never said anything in those terrible times and just pretended it was all an ongoing perplexity. If he did know about it and did nothing, then of course he would be risking his own livelihood and his own family. And who would do that?

Then one day, out of the blue, totally unexpectedly, the Game Warden died.

The church was packed, I'm told, when my Grandfather walked in. It got extremely quiet as he walked up to the coffin. He was wearing not only a suit but a tie...and no one, ever, had seen him in anything but patched, raggedy coveralls. In fact, I don't believe he ever wore a suit again until the day of my Grandmother's funeral.

He stopped at the side of the coffin and leaned down over the body of his enemy. He whispered something that no one could make out. Then he turned around and at the front of the Church, facing the congregation, broke down and wept uncontrollably.

Chapter Nine

"I know of no way of judging the future but by the past" Patrick Henry.

"Some people come into our life as a blessing, while others come into our life as a lesson, so love them for who they are instead of judging them for who they are not" Yolanda Hadid

I was a bit surprised at the overall reaction to the previous piece I wrote about my Grandfather. The most common reaction was that he should have been at best kept away from kids; at worst locked up. Perhaps that is true...but then again, perhaps not.

The Day My Grandfather Was Tagged As A Psychopath

It's pretty clear a lot of people think my Grandfather was a psychopath.

They came to this conclusion after reading about how he shot a dog in front of two small children, one of whom was me. Prior to writing the article, it had not occurred to me, but I suppose such an awful thing does today seem like the act of a psychopath.

But today is not back then. Back then, there was no penicillin, no antibiotics; they were not available or had not been invented yet. If you cut yourself, or stepped on a nail, or were exposed to a "social disease," you would probably start to die and there would be nothing anyone could do to save you. There was no 911, even if you had a phone which most did not. FDR's safety net was not in place yet: there was no social security, no Medicare and no FDIC. If your bank went bust, and thousands did, you instantly lost every dime you had put in and it was irrecoverable. There were no social services, no food banks, no public assistance, no crop insurance, no health insurance, no disability. There were no jobs either, so no money could be had for smoothing life's rough edges.

So back then what you had to do, as a dust-bowl era farmer in the depression of the 1930s, to watch out for your family and what your available options were, well, it was different than now. Unimaginably different. Different like this:

On that day, two of my grandparents' young children had walked down the long, farm driveway to the main road, heading out to a distant pasture.

The two little girls had not been gone for long when my grandfather and my grandmother saw the horizon line of a Black Blizzard bearing down. Black Blizzards, they called them then, and Black Tornadoes. They would approach at terrible speeds, usually outpacing a person and often arriving faster than an old farm car could go. The dust storms of the thirties were cruel, burying farms, crops, animals and dreams. And they were killers.

Sighting that storm was a moment so looming with dread and the prospect of unthinkable catastrophe, that my Grandmother trembled years later to tell me of it. There was no one else to help. If one of their parents didn't go and try and find them, those two young girls would surely die. If one of them did go, the odds were that that person would die as well. And they had four other children. The immutable sentence for a farm family if one of the parents vanished was destruction.

My Grandfather's name was Clayton. "Clayt," was all my Grandmother could bring herself to say to him, "Clayt."

He pulled three winter scarves from their old bureau. His he wrapped around his face. His girls' scarves he stuffed into the bib of his overalls. They were their only scarves, to be brought forth once yearly upon the arrival of South Dakota's winter.

My Grandfather ran down their long, long driveway towards the main road. He raced that dust storm for the prize of his little girls. And he lost. As he reached the main road, the storm fell upon them all, howling and shrieking, black as ink.

"Dust storm winds were clocked at (as much as) 60 mph " "...the impact is like a shovelful of fine sand flung against the face," "...People caught in their own yards grope for the doorstep. it was just like shutting a barn door. It was that dark, that black...." "...chickens (would go) to roost in the middle of the day, because the dust storm made it so dark the chickens thought it was night." The New Republic, History.com, american-historama.org, Herman Goertzen, Avis D. Carlson.

My Grandfather followed the direction his girls had taken. He did so by stumbling through ditches while continually grabbing roadside fences with his right hand as he went seeking his children in the darkness of the storm. It was the only way to keep himself oriented. The fences were barbed wire.

It was quite impossible for him to find his children, in that howling blackness. Impossible. But find them he did, and all he would say about it later was "I heard them." But they were across the road, beaten down by the storm. He could not possibly have heard them, or seen them either for that matter.

"I was so proud of them" my Grandfather told me years later. "They remembered what I told them. 'if you ever get caught in a dust storm find a culvert. Then, lay down in the ditch and put your head into the culvert so you can breathe.' "

His daughters remembered his advice but encountered a problem. The culvert was only big enough for one. They were dying in that ditch when my Grandfather found them. They were feebly fighting with each other, not to stick their own head in the culvert, but to force their sister to do so. They were 9 and 11 years old.

He wrapped their faces in those old, winter scarves, turned around and headed for home. One of his children he slung over his back. The other he carried in the crook of his arm. Home and safety lay in the opposite direction from which he had come, so my Grandfather used his other hand to grip the fences and their barbs so he could stumble back through ditch after ditch. To fall, to lose the way was to die.

He finally came upon their mailbox, which was at the head of the long driveway to the farm house. He later made light of it. "Once I was there I just went up to the house."

But there was no fence along the driveway to guide him. My grandmother heard rhythmic banging on their front door. When she flung it open, she found my grandfather lying on the doorstep, after having crawled up the driveway. On his back was one of his girls, my Aunt, who went on to have 5 kids of her own. Crooked in one arm was his youngest girl, my mom. Later, my Grandmother found on that door a dozen, apple-sized blood smears left from the heel of the barb torn hand he had used to pound on the farm house door.

Years later, my parents lived in Minnesota, only a couple hour's drive away from the old farmstead in South Dakota. My Grandfather came to my parents place one day to see a doctor for some check-up or another. My Grandmother had passed away a few years earlier. Grandfather had mellowed a lot, taking delight in listening to his beloved Dodgers and passing out sweets to his great grandkids. I dropped by to say hello.

I was almost through college by then (my brother and I were the first ever on both sides of our families to go and then to graduate). I found that my Grandfather and I struggled to find common conversational ground, and that our exchanges often just dribbled away. Finally, we sat in silence in my parents small living room and stared out at the wintry landscape.

"Hey," I said finally. "would you like to go see some fish?"

"Dead fish?" He asked, clearly unexcited.

I assured him that the fish were indeed alive and there were a lot of them. They were all beautifully hued, I enthused, and could be seen in Glass tanks which allowed for close-up views.

Off we went. He later tried to assure my mother that I had

neglected to mention that the fish tanks in question were a major draw of the Aquarium Bar in Fargo, North Dakota. Fargo, now having achieved some movie fame, was then a small town just across the river from my parents' home in Moorhead, Minnesota.

I don't remember all of the specifics of that afternoon of fish watching, but I do remember it as a wonderful time. When we finally wandered back to the house some hours later, my mother was livid.

"You... you..." she sputtered at her father, as he and I groggily held onto each other.

"Now, Sis," responded Granddad, using his pet name for her in the vain hope, I believe, of softening her up. It didn't work. She peremptorily ordered him to bed (but did bring him dinner later). She then turned her wrath on me.

She gave me a blistering lecture on the dangers inherent in such an afternoon, responsibility, youth versus age and many other things which thankfully now have pretty much passed into the mists of time. She forgave her father almost immediately but glaringly brought up that afternoon with me for many years thereafter.

It was worth it.

CHAPTER TEN

"The ideal condition would be, I admit, that men should be right by instinct, but since we are all likely to go astray, the reasonable thing is to learn from those who can teach" Sophocles

"Experience is a dear teacher, and only fools will learn from no other" Benjamin Franklin

It seemed to be part of the ethos when my Grandfather was raised, that you didn't directly tell people what to do. He did occasionally make exceptions, however—

The Day I Got A Beating From My Grandfather

The world-renowned anthropologist, Margaret Mead, (1901-1978) opined after the initial moon landing that for the first time in human history children could not look to their elders for guidance as to how to deal with the future. And in many respects, I do believe that's true. Hardly any of us raise livestock for our own family's food or subsistence hunt any more. We mostly forage in grocery stores, and butcher by cutting open the plastic wrap around our food. And we're pretty much the better for it. Pretty much.

My Grandfather only beat me once.

It was at the end of a long day. I was tired and I was hungry. I don't remember what we'd been doing from dawn onwards that day, but it was something in the fields. There were still animals to feed, which was one of my assigned chores, but I thought some supper and a few minutes of rest would make that endeavor a bit less onerous.

I pulled a chair up to the table and reached for the bread. My grandfather looked at me. "Have you fed the animals yet?" he asked mildly. I replied in the negative.

Suddenly I found myself lying on floor, head ringing from what must've been a mighty slap. The next thing I knew he picked me up, none too gently, and kicked open the back door. The back door was connected to what we laughingly called "The Porch." "The Porch" was really just a small wooden square above a couple of steps leading down into the barnyard. Granddad had put it in so my grandmother could simply walk out the back door and throw over periodic offerings to the pigs. It was also the launch point for potato peels and various meal scraps provided daily to the constant delight and attention of the chickens.

I landed face down in the latest throw to the pigs; a thin veneer of something wet lying over a blanket of chicken crap that had been built up over the course of the summer months. My grandfather was shouting at me. "you never eat before feeding the animals! Never!"

His shouts followed me into the night as I ran for the barn. "They can't feed themselves; they depend on you. You hear me? THEY DEPEND ON YOU!"

I fed the animals then returned to the house. By this time, I was more tired, more hungry, and quite terrified. It had become dark. We all retired early on my Grandad's farm, bone weary from the efforts of the day. Everyone had gone to bed except my Grandfather who was waiting up for me.

"Did you feed all the animals?" he asked. When I replied yes he ordered me to sit down at the table. He then handed me a full dinner plate which he had obviously set aside. This was no small feat in a house full of hungry, hard-working people. He waited until I finished, then asked me if I wanted something more. When I said no, he nodded once and without another word went to bed.

When I told the story years later to one my Uncles, he stared off into the distance and allowed as how he'd gotten beaten by my Granddad, his father, only once as well. They were pheasant hunting. None of the other kids were along. My Uncle, ten at the time, was alone, hunting for the first time with his dad; a true rite of passage in South Dakota. My Uncle was carrying an old 410 shotgun my granddad had scrounged up from somewhere; as broke as they continually were this was no mean accomplishment. With much ceremony, he had given the gun to his son, my Uncle, on the eve of their first pheasant hunt together.

They were walking in corn stubble when a pheasant burst up immediately in front. My Uncle was so excited he shot at it instantly. And hit it. Unfortunately, they were so close together, my Uncle and his first pheasant, that the poor bird was basically blown to pieces.

My Uncle told me that the next thing he knew my grandfather had grabbed his gun and thrown it out of sight into the cornfield. He said he didn't remember much of what happened after that, although it was unpleasant and painful. What he did remember, he said, was my Grandfather screaming at him "You didn't give it a chance! You didn't give it a chance! YOU ALWAYS GIVE THEM A CHANCE." It was another year before my grandfather would take him hunting again.

My grandfather used to give me advice and comments as I grew older, all of which I ignored as it didn't ever seem to apply to anything I was experiencing. One time, after college and just into new work in California, he asked me what I did exactly. I went into what was almost certainly mind-numbing detail about creating commercials and commercial sound tracks. "That's all very fine," he responded when I ran down. "But don't you work?"

My Uncle is gone now. Before he passed, one of the many things he did was teach young kids about hunting and gun safety. "I was really mad at my Dad for awhile about the pheasant thing," he told me before he got so sick. "But for years I've told kids to always give the animals they hunt a chance. Just seems like the right thing to do."

For my part, I hated the farm and never wanted to repeat any part of it, including the good parts. I don't even root in flower beds and am always resistant to mowing the lawn. But I have had a lot of animals and pets pretty much continuously over the years. Each day, my animals always eat first. They depend on me, you see.

CHAPTER ELEVEN

"Airplanes may kill you, but they ain't likely to hurt you"
Satchel Paige.

"Guys would sleep with a bicycle if it had the right color lip gloss on. They have no shame. They're like bull elks in a field" Tori Amos

If you're at an age when the following episode makes sense to you, there's no Life Lesson to be had here.

The Day I had a Hot Date and We Fell Out of the Sky

A hot date and two cases of beer was all it had taken to get us into this mess. That and the completely unauthorized use of a military snowplow.

When the roads were clear, it was a 5-hour winter's drive from my airbase in North Dakota to Minneapolis where a lady friend had taken up residence. After a rather breathy invitation, a New Year's Eve party in Minneapolis beckoned. Actually, it did more than beckon...it shouted with the irresistible siren call that only the young and on the hunt can truly hear. Problem was that while New Year's Eve day dawned clear, the night before a blizzard had come through depositing feet of snow. Roads were closed in all directions.

I was in the Air National Guard at the time, stationed at an airport in mid-North Dakota. The airport was part civilian, part military. It was blazingly hot in the summer. This was balanced by it being cold as hell in the winter, with armpit deep snow. More often than not, this snow was deposited by ferocious blizzards which would build huge drifts and effectively drop temperatures to 30 below zero.

The airport's runways were snow-blocked as well as the roads that morning, but I went up to the tower anyway. At that time, hitch-hiking was not considered a sure way to meet a serial killer. Better yet, some wag had come up with the successful idea of occasionally scoring a hitch on a private plane. That's of course if you didn't mind hanging out at an airport until you found an amenable pilot and didn't care where, exactly, you landed.

I figured it was worth a shot. To my surprise, when I walked in to the tower's connected "ready room," there were two guys looking at a flight plan log and arguing about flying to Minneapolis.

One of them, the older one, had a broken-veined, red face and a sparse comb over. The younger guy was being a real dick, whining about getting to Minneapolis for New Year's Eve and clearly implying that it was the other one's fault they were stuck.

The older guy was beyond exasperated. "The runways are blocked with snow; what the hell do you expect me to do?"

Ah. I walked up to them and allowed as how I might be able to solve that problem, my price being to hitch a ride on their flight to Minneapolis. They blinked at me. "Sure," said the comb over guy.

I called my buddy Sargent Johnson, who was initially skeptical due to a couple of schemes gone badly awry in the past. He was in charge of a lot of the base's military vehicles including snowplows.

I explained my plan. "No!" he responded instantly. "Goddamn it, no! That's unauthorized use of military equipment and I won't do it! Besides, what's in it for me?"

Short negotiations resulted in a two cases of beer commitment on my side. Ten minutes later my new traveling companions and I were treated to the sight of a huge snowplow, military off-green, clearing the small craft runway we needed to use. The blizzard had not hit Minneapolis, so once airborne we were good in the sense that we could land upon arrival.

My new companions were astonished, delighted. Their 6-seater Cessna was tied down outside a hangar and had, apparently, weathered the storm quite well. "Give us 5 minutes. Then, come on out and hop aboard."

Hop aboard I did. Mr. Comb-Over fired up the engine and we took off, they whooping with delight and me congratulating myself for being so damn tricky.

A few minutes later, I wasn't feeling quite so damn tricky.

"Just fly the plane! Dad, PLEASE! PLEASE! JUST FLY THE FUCKING PLANE!"

The older guy was shouting incoherently and beating on the plane's dashboard. The younger guy, riding shotgun in the Cessna was, it seemed, his son.

Sitting in back I kept thinking how quiet things were between the shouts. Not surprising, since our only engine had shut down. We had been flying along smugly harmonizing off-color verses to "Row, Row, Row Your Boat." Then in an instant we became a winged rock.

"There, there!" shouted the son pointing, "on the left, on the left, there's a flat field!" Since our landing gear was fixed like a 3-wheeled tricycle, if the selected snow-covered field wasn't flat as a board we were well and truly screwed. A belly landing was not an option. We couldn't see any roads, which might have provided salvation. This being the case, I decided that right then was probably not the time to mention snow usually covered deep furrows on many of the fields, the furrows having been humped up by farmers harvesting the last of the sugar beet crop.

A Mayday was called. And called again. It was pretty clear we were going in.

"Son, I'm so sorry. I'm so sorry. I'm sorry." The son did not respond. He now sat silently; fixedly staring out the side window as we went down. Our weeping pilot started cursing, screaming, mashing the key in the starter again and again only to hear the engine grind.

I swear to God we were just a few feet off the deck when the engine emitted a loud chuff and a bang! and fired right up.

We flew back to our starting point. The engine would stutter occasionally. "C'mon, you bitch, c'mon, c'mon!" the pilot kept muttering. His hands were trembling on the yoke. When the airport came in sight, the son reached out and covered his Dad's shaking hands with his own.

We landed without further incident.

"That stupid asshole should be dead." I was standing next to the plane. It was now hangared and being looked over by a mechanic, who had just rendered his opinion of the pilot. We both gazed through the window at Mr. Comb Over's car weaving uncertainly out of the airport.

"Well, I'm glad he's not." I responded, deeply sincere. "Why do you say that?"

"I was watching when he was getting ready to leave." The mechanic shook his head. "The dumb shit didn't pre-flight check his plane. He just had a couple of other idiots jump in and they took off."

"So?" I responded. Not being a pilot myself, I added "It must have been 20 below outside; can hardly blame the guy."

The mechanic glared over, clearly moving me from his "O.K. Guy" into his "Idiot" mental column.

"His fucking plane sat out in a blizzard all night. I guarantee you the engine compartment got packed with show. The engine got hot; the snow melted and screwed up the engine's electrical. What a dipshit. He's lucky he's not scattered all over the ground...along with his two buddies."

"Yes," I agreed. "Lucky indeed."

When I got back to the airport a bit later after a sojourn to purchase the two cases of payment beer, I found that the clearing of the small craft runway had opened an opportunity for a number of other small craft pilots who also wanted to get to Minneapolis that day.

All the newly gathered pilots were buzzing about the highly unusual Mayday call; shaking their heads over what did indeed turn out to be the reason for it. When I announced I had been on the plane but not the pilot, I got multiple offers for a ride-along to Minneapolis. A few hours later I found myself at the party. And there, looking beautiful, as I recall, was my lady friend.

She took my hands. "I'm so glad you came. I didn't think you'd be able to make it, what with the blizzard. Did you have any trouble getting here?"

"Not a bit," I responded.

CHAPTER TWELVE

"Home may be where the heart is but it's no place to spend Wednesday afternoon" Walker Percy

"I love my small town...but I could not have stayed there. No way" Jeremy Renner

If you grow up in a small town, the time may come for you to leave, to find a future elsewhere. It's a big move, a Life Event. Plan carefully.

The Day We Blew Town with the Monkey

I hated the monkey and the monkey hated me.

I cannot tell you why I hated the monkey. It might have been because the monkey repeatedly pissed in my bed. Or it might have been because the monkey pulled down my bookshelves and then crapped on the debris. I really don't know.

The monkey hated me unreservedly. Why this was so, I also find perplexing. I never pissed on the monkey's bed, nor did I ever crap on the monkey's possessions. I did, however, always cut the monkey off after two beers, so perhaps that was it.

If you ever acquire a pet or, God forbid, a Roommate and you are told they have a prehensile anything, run away. The loose definition of "prehensile" is an appendage capable of grasping. The term generally is applied to an appendage you would not normally think was capable of grasping. Such as a long, hairy tail. So if you have, for example, a Spider Monkey with a prehensile tail in your environment, what you really have is a grudge holding beast that can wreak havoc with two "hands," two grasping feet and a tail. All at the same time. Plus Spider Monkeys have a huge bladder, the output of which it seems they can control at will. Or not.

I did not acquire the monkey initially. Initially I acquired a Roommate. The Roommate was a college chum who was a bit down on his luck. I offered to let him sleep free in my basement, which he did. His possessions slowly began to fill up the house. One day I arrived home to find a huge empty cage sitting in and dominating my small living room.

My Roommate was missing so I could not demand an explanation, although the next day when a monkey appeared in the cage I felt some conversation was in order.

I remember the discussion as being one of rescue and the monetary value of a Spider Monkey, in the unlikely event I had wished to buy one. The monkey had apparently been acquired for free, which should've been a dead giveaway that something was seriously amiss. There was also a broad hint from my Roommate regarding lab experiments on living animals. The college we both had attended was Liberal Arts. It did not occur to me at the time to check on which of my philosophy professors was in the process of carrying out a plan to vivisect a monkey, thus requiring an intervention and rescue on our part.

Things started amiably enough. My Roommate named the monkey "Cheetah," a nod, I guess, to multiple Saturday afternoons spent watching old black and white Tarzan movies. I always felt "Cheetah" was a stupid name, like naming a dog "Spot."

I do have to admit that initially Cheetah made us quite popular; a monkey in Minnesota being a tad unusual. At first, we got a lot of free drinks because of the monkey, which my Roommate would carry around inside of his thick, winter coat. The monkey would stick its head out of the coat by undoing the middle button. This self-learned trick should have been a warning to us all.

The Monkey In A Coat Ploy earned a lot of "awwwww" comments from young ladies we would encounter in our favorite bar, along with agreements to come home with us to see the monkey in its natural habitat.

All went well until one night, in the bar, something spooked the monkey. I learned later that screeching at the top of its simian lungs, the monkey sprang from my Roommate's coat. It then ran up and down the bar, spilling drinks and throwing everything within reach of its little hands, feet, and prehensile tail. As it started knocking over liquor bottles on the back bar, the monkey anointed the bottles and all patrons within range with a fine mist of monkey pee. As my Roommate told me later, he and the monkey were both ejected from the bar amidst incoherent shouting about liquor licenses and the health department. Part of the shouting, I was led to believe, involved cries of "never come back or we will have you both arrested!" "Both," I assumed being my Roommate and Cheetah, although I was never quite clear under what statute the monkey would be busted.

This episode caused us to spend more recreational hours at home which is when the trouble really started.

We started hosting" "Game Nights." A "game night" consisted of a group of invitees playing a board game called Acquire. We would fuel these evenings with copious amounts of home-cooked popcorn and free-flowing beer. The beer was, we felt, one of our most important discoveries. It was called Chief Oshkosh Beer, a Wisconsin product, and sold for the princely sum of $1.25 an eight pack. To our delight and amazement, on a per bottle basis this made Chief Oshkosh Beer cheaper than Coca-Cola.

The monkey, as it turned out, loved both food groups. We quit serving popcorn in a communal bucket as people started objecting to eating popcorn covered with monkey spit. We then had to begin warning gamers to keep an eye on their beer. The monkey would seize any open beer bottle it could find, preferably one as full as possible. It would then wrap both arms, both legs and its prehensile tail around the stubby, brown bottle, lay on its back, and chug all the contents. Based on relative body size, this was probably the equivalent of a human being sucking down 2 or 3 gallons of beer without stopping.

It quickly became apparent that after a couple bottles of Chief Oshkosh, Cheetah became even more unmanageable. Plus, the beer seemed to bring on a bit of a bladder control problem, which is to say a problem worse than was normally the case. I took to cutting off the monkey's beer supply after two purloined bottles. I would then banish the monkey, which by this time would be quite surly, to its cage. I now firmly believe that my ongoing interruptions of the monkey's benders was the root cause of its continuing enmity.

At any rate, I had already decided to leave the Midwest for California. I had exchanged my car for a van and was in the process of liquidating everything I could to raise cash for the journey. My Roommate and his girlfriend decided they would come along for the ride. They would, they said, spring for a few tanks of gas, plus share expenses, if we could make a slight detour to Boston. It seems the girlfriend wanted to reconnect with someone she knew who had a job there and promised to find her work. As that someone was also an ex-girlfriend of mine, I didn't feel the multi – thousand mile detour was a deal killer. There was one item, however that was a real poser:

"We have to take the monkey."

I could not believe my Roommate was serious. I hated even walking by the monkey's cage, still in my living room. The thought of spending days with the monkey in a van was almost too much to contemplate. Then again the extra money and expense split was enormously appealing.

It almost became a self-solving problem. My Roommate was quite lax about snapping the padlock shut on the monkey's cage door. This was a problem, since if there was no lock in place the monkey was adept at opening its cage door. From the inside.

With just a few days to go before the beginning of our journey and the monkey question still unresolved, my Roommate and I arrived at my house one afternoon to find the padlock dangling open on the cage door, which was also open. There was no monkey in sight.

We scoured the house high and low. The monkey was not pulling down bookshelves or curled up in my bed where it liked to nap under the covers and pee without moving. We looked everywhere. No monkey. My Roommate was becoming more distressed by the moment. "Why," I thought to myself "he actually likes the stupid thing."

Spurred on by guilt at feeling so happy, I redoubled my search efforts. No luck. "Well it's gone" I said cheerfully. "I'm sure it will be okay," I added, trying not to look out the window at the frosty, Minnesota winter landscape.

I recalled there were a few stray bottles of Chief Oshkosh in the fridge. Obviously, beer was the only fix for my Roommate's sorrow. I popped open the refrigerator door. And there was the damn monkey.

It was shaking so hard from cold you could also almost hear its teeth rattle. Its stomach was distended from eating everything in the fridge it could stuff down along with biting hunks out of everything else. In one hand the monkey was holding a head of badly chewed lettuce. In the other, a much-bitten tomato. Its prehensile tail was wrapped around a bottle of beer, which fortunately it had been unable to open in spite of extensive chewing on the bottle cap. It had also peed on our stash of day old pizza. This was a sin comparable to desecrating heaven sent mana, not to mention the ruination of our dinner.

"Here's your beer!" I said heartily, slamming the refrigerator door shut. Unfortunately, I was not quick enough. "Cheetah!" My Roommate screamed. He then extracted the monkey from the refrigerator. Even with salvation at hand, the monkey held tightly to its stolen head of lettuce and the remnants of our last tomato.

My Roommate performed monkey first aid by basking it in the warm breeze of a hairdryer. This proved to be a mistake also. The monkey loved the hairdryer experience so much, it took to demanding repeats, often dragging the hairdryer across the floor searching for a victim. Once found, the monkey would "ook" at the poor soul chosen for duty. The next hour would then have to be spent warming the monkey. It was either that or get bitten if the initial, plaintive ooking was ineffectual. This whole much-repeated scenario moved from endearing to old instantly.

The day of our departure arrived. We had not discussed the monkey further after its near-death experience. I had the van keys in hand. My Roommate and his girlfriend were in the van. So was the monkey. I swear I would've left it behind had not my Roommate's girlfriend guaranteed she would hold it in her lap the whole way. That lasted about 20 miles right up until the monkey's persistent bladder problem reasserted itself.

After the first day on the road, we found we had to do all of our eating in the van. The monkey had quickly found a favorite perch on the steering wheel. As we drove along, the monkey would wrap all of its appendages around the wheel as it sat on top. Thus secured, it would gently rock back and forth for miles, seemingly in a road trip trance of some sort. Unfortunately, this also put the monkey in a position to discover the horn button in the center of the steering wheel.

The first time we stopped to get something to eat, we left the monkey in the van. As we sat in the restaurant, we suddenly heard a horn begin to blare nonstop (this was prior to the advent of car alarms). Then a young boy came running into the restaurant. "There's a monkey in a van outside!" he shouted, clearing out the restaurant. The monkey turned out to be able to draw quite a crowd. They even took pictures. Being no slouch, the monkey quickly learned that all it needed to do to bring its pack mates back to the van was to sit unmoving on the horn button.

A few days later, we rolled into Boston. The van, unsurprisingly, smelled heavily of monkey.

My Roommate and I found a very small apartment. We were able to rent it, probably because we neglected to mention the monkey. My Roommate's girlfriend moved in with the lady she had come to see. She did indeed find a job as hoped, so that trip goal was achieved. Along with our clothes and the monkey, the van was loaded with cases of liquid soap. My Roommate and I had gotten involved with a multilevel scheme involving home cleaning products. Unfortunately, this get rich quick scenario was not well received in Boston.

As we made the rounds hawking soap, my Roommate had his girlfriend babysit the monkey at their place. This babysitting of the monkey unavoidably involved my ex-girlfriend who had originally rented the apartment. Soon their landlord was dropping by, citing reports of shrieking in the building that sounded like a child was being tortured. We were quickly informed that babysitting the monkey was no longer an option.

Once we had taken the monkey back in full-time, our landlord was even less understanding. He just didn't want to hear about it. "Either that noise quits or you do. Now."

We were light on soap appointments for the day. My Roommate asked if he could borrow the van. He came home to the monkey and I that night, quite somber. Next morning, promising only to be gone for an hour or two, he took the monkey and drove off in the van. A couple of hours later he was back, with the van and without the monkey.

"Okay I'll bite," I said. "Where is that beer swilling little S.O.B.?"

"Cheetah is in a happier place," he replied. God in heaven. I felt the blood drain from my face. I hated the monkey, but I hadn't wanted it murdered.

He must have read my expression. "No, no! I didn't kill it. I couldn't do that. I gave Cheetah to a television station in Boston." He went on to explain that the TV station hosted a live, daily children's show. They could not, he said, believe their luck to actually have gotten a live monkey. He further swore that he did not receive a dime for the transaction, but thereafter he started picking up meals and bar tabs. I found this delightful, but highly suspicious in light of his adamant position that he had not sold the monkey into servitude.

It was not long thereafter until we had to admit the soap business was a bust. We disposed of our inventory, partially with the help of a dumpster.

My Roommate got a job in Rhode Island. I picked up a couple of fellow travelers from Boston College to join me on my journey to California. The hefty fee to them for coast to coast transportation was four tanks of gas. One of my passengers was a bearded, gangly lad. He brought with him a small backpack and a sitar, on which he twanged nonstop all the way from Boston to Kansas City where I dropped him off. My other passenger was a young lady who smoked a lot of dope while gazing rapturously at the sitar player. She joined family in San Bernardino, leaving me alone when I rolled into Los Angeles.

I later received a message from my ex-girlfriend. She related that the monkey was appearing daily on Boston TV. "At least one of you made it here in Boston," her message read, which I felt was kind of harsh. She closed by mentioning that the TV station had announced they were going to rename the show after the monkey.

They did change the monkey's name. To Oscar.

CHAPTER THIRTEEN

"There's no business like show business, but there are several businesses like accounting" David Letterman

Show business, reputation to the contrary, is as random as everything else. A lot of people I've met or read about who are in the industry speak of how being involved with show business saved them. Well, it saved me too, I guess, but not quite in the same way they talk about.

The Day I Was Saved by Mickey Mouse

She was undoubtedly stoned to the gills.

She was riding around on the circular luggage delivery system in the baggage Area of the San Francisco airport. She would hand a flower to every passenger she passed, all of whom were looking at her in complete bafflement. Grinning hugely as she circulated around with the growing mound of luggage, she kept handing out flowers until they were all gone. The flowers were daisies. She was beautiful, in that breath-taking, coltish way young women have.

We weren't so different in age. I just stood there, having been sent to California by the insurance agency I worked for to deliver a death claim check.

I looked down at myself in my suit and tie and thought morosely of the task at hand. I looked across at her, shrieking with delight in her tie-dye. "My God," I thought to myself. "Am I going to allow all of this to just pass me by?"

I quit my insurance job and bought a van. Shortly thereafter, I left Minnesota forever, accompanied by two friends and a monkey, all of us loose inside. I desperately wanted to go to California so we drove to Boston, where we all went broke and the monkey became a TV star. I seem to recall that the Boston detour had something to do with a lady. Four months later, without my friends and thankfully without the monkey, I drove the van to California.

My one and only contact in California had graduated from the same Minnesota college as I two years earlier with a degree in Theater Arts. He had parlayed that into a job working a spotlight at the live Disney on Parade show in Anaheim, California. I had graduated college with a degree in political science. This qualified me to take a shot at exactly nothing involving productions of any kind whatsoever. Still, I called him and let him know I had blown into Los Angeles. He rather sadly informed me that he did not have any suggestions as to what I could do to keep body and soul together.

About a month later, I had just begun the process of starving in California, when my friend excitedly called. It seemed he thought he could help me get a job for the remaining six weeks of the live Disney on Parade show "working off the Call Board." He explained that the Stagehands' Union controlled all the jobs on live productions. Hiring of stagehands always favored Union members and their offspring. However, once in a while all slots could not be filled with union members. In such cases, there were openings on the "Call Board;" slang for the listing of needed stage hand workers on a particular show. Non-union Call Board workers had to be pre-approved by the Union Steward.

There was an opening on the Disney on Parade Call Board. It was for a stagehand electrician. He had, he said, recommended me highly and I had an interview that day.

The Union Steward looked like an ex-boxer. A very dirty T-shirt held up a spectacular belly.

"Yeah?" he said to begin the interview. "You here for the electrician slot?"

Now, this guy was really intimidating. "Yes," I stammered, "but I don't know anything about..."

"Like I give a shit?" He responded." You can stick a plug into a socket, right?" When I nodded in affirmation, he looked over his shoulder. "Jake!" he shouted. "Tell those idiots over at the Mouse House to get off my ass. I just filled the roster for the show."

Then he stood aside. I had the job. I was about to meet John the drunken Wire Man, Alice and her dour stage mother, the three, gay Little Pigs, Hal the homophobe, a grumpy Cinderella and a guy who kept getting lost in the curtains who had been dubbed The Creature.

Everyone went out of their way to say hello, at least on the stagehand side. There was an immutable pecking order in place; dancers and actors were at the top. They would occasionally issue orders to us, quickly countermanded by the Union Steward, but otherwise did not mingle.

John was a short, rangy guy with huge calloused hands. A miasma of whiskey fumes rolled before him as he walked up. "I'm John. I am the Wire Man. Always bet on me." Initially I thought the term "bet on me" was a general sort of boast that he would always get the job done. His position was a really dangerous and important one. His job as Wire Man was to set up and connect all the steel cables required for overhead lighting and acrobatic work. Trapeze and high wire acts were not part of that particular Disney show, except for a circus "pole man" who played Peter Pan. He did so by dressing all in green, including really tight green tights and a green hat with an oversized green feather in it. On cue, he would climb up and weave back and forth at the top of a long, long pole. He always lost the hat but took to dressing as Peter Pan off performance as well as on.

After his greeting and gambling instructions, in an amazing show of strength Wire Man John climbed hand over hand up a steel cable until he was a fly spec against the ceiling. I noticed a group of other stagehands bunching up to watch. I thought their mesmerized gaze was from awe similar to mine, until I noticed they were actually betting. One side was wagering that John would climb down on his own. The other side was betting he would arrive back down on the floor, but with a full gravity assist.

The wagering seesawed back and forth, depending on each bettor's assessment of how drunk John was on that particular day. He never fell, and I never placed a bet either way. The betting on Wire Man John stopped, never to resume, after he showed up for work one day beaten up pretty badly. To his credit, the union steward ordered him to go home, but Wire Man went up anyway and did his work. This earned him enormous respect and admiration, putting to an end to the rather macabre daily pool regarding his life expectancy. Later that day, I asked him what had transpired to result in his receiving a beating. He ruefully explained that the night before, he had gone to a bar where patrons could get two for one drinks. The promotional proviso was that they had to use a bar provided seatbelt and strap themselves to their bar stool. "I did that," said Wire Man. "And then a guy comes up and starts hitting me! Every time he hits me, it spins the stool around so I can't unfasten the Goddamn seatbelt and hit him back."

A really good looking, young blonde lady walked by, dressed exactly like Alice in Wonderland. She was closely followed by a very stern faced older lady. "Hello," I said, I thought pleasantly. The older lady stepped in front of the Alice person. "Come." She said to her and they marched off together. Laughter erupted from the other stagehands. "Consider yourself lucky," said one. "At least you didn't get cursed at." I was then informed that the older lady was a rather classical stage mother, who was determined that not only that her young daughter be a star, but that she would emerge from her Disney experience unsullied. I don't know if the stage mom, or Alice, was ultimately successful in either goal. The role of Alice, however, was extremely demanding with a lot of running around chasing the White Rabbit and escaping from the Red Queen in front of the audience. One time, Alice was sick for a day and her understudy took over. Between scenes, the understudy would alternate between trying to catch her breath and throwing up into a wastebasket.

Then, the Three Little Pigs wandered by. Actually, it was three very musclebound guys, each wearing a huge, fiberglass combination pig head and torso. In a time when not just the United States but the whole world was packed into a closet, these guys were defiantly and outspokenly gay. Although they were actors, they regularly crossed the actor/stagehand divide with compliments for us. They were quite well-liked by almost everyone and not just because no one wanted to mess with them as they spent most of their off-hours pumping iron at Golds Gym, something not much in vogue then.

I say "liked by almost everyone," as there was one notable exception: an extremely homophobic stagehand, whose job it was to push around the Three Pigs' House of Bricks prop during the Three Pigs skit. In order to do this, he had to be inside the prop house. With the Three Pigs. He also had to work the "boxing glove on a pole" that would emerge from the prop house to hit the villainous wolf.

This guy, Hal (not his real name), it was unanimously agreed, was a real jerk. He started making a lot of anti-gay remarks and telling homophobic jokes, until everyone adopted a policy of either immediately walking away or telling him to shut the hell up. The Three Pigs took it, I thought, with aplomb but one day apparently reached a breaking point.

The stage manager sensed trouble. Each of the pig head costumes cost thousands of dollars to create and was one-of-a-kind, he announced. Punching a hole in any one of them would be a really bad idea, job wise. Besides, everyone's real goal wasn't to fight, but to get rid of The Jerk. Unfortunately, he was a union guy and almost impossible to get fired, unless he committed a heinous act such as punching a divot in one of the pig costumes. With an actor in it.

The Three Pigs clearly decided Hal had to go. Soon it became apparent they had further determined that victory lay in psychological warfare.

It quickly became a show within a show. Soon, at every performance all we stagehands, and later many other people who appeared from God knows where, would gather just before the Pig House prop was pushed on stage by Hal, who was inside with the three actors in full pig costume. I found myself wishing I could sell tickets.

As soon as the door closed on the Pig House, the three actors playing the Pigs would start in badgering their nemesis. They were hilarious. Using falsetto voices, they would loudly begin discussing Hal's various physical attributes and sexual prowess, or lack thereof. They would also critically and graphically review Hal's activities and performance at totally imaginary gay parties, always held the night before. I won't repeat any of it here except to say that based on the noise emanating from the Pig House, I suspect the conversations included some goosing as well as extraordinarily, politically and at the time, socially incorrect propositions and discussions.

Hal continued to show up to work for some days after battle was joined, but each time he appeared he was drunker than the last.

Finally, one night he was so loaded he could hardly walk. The Pig House careened on stage with a new level of internal uproar now clearly audible to many in the audience. At the point where a boxing glove on a stick was to hit the wolf, it was pushed out with such force that the boxing glove and the thick wooden dowel it was attached to left the Pig House like a rocket. The entire assembly clattered onto the stage floor, having been ripped from its moorings by the force of the push, undoubtedly by Hal.

The audience loved it. Hal never showed up for work again.

Early on, I had been assigned very specific duties. Those were to plug in the battery packs on the dancers' costumes which were festooned with little lights, and to walk behind props as they were pushed on stage. Walking behind various props, my job was to carry an electrical cord with a plug on one end, which I was to plug into a socket on the stage floor between acts. At that time, the

Stagehands' Union was divided into very specific areas, which is say into "electrical work," props, carpentry, and so forth. Each division was rigidly enforced, so much so that I was chewed out one time for putting my hand on a prop to help push it onstage when it got hung up. I was not part of that area of responsibility, so I was to "keep my damn hands to myself" and just carry the plug.

The moment arrived on my first day for the first performance of the day in front of an audience. There were two sets of stage curtains to be pulled back to get the show underway. One curtain was very heavy and was opened and closed by a motor. The other, a light interior curtain, was opened by hand.

The curtains opened. As the applause swelled and the dancers glided onstage, I noticed that there was a lump in the curtains where they had been drawn back, said lump emitting strange mewling noises.

The Stage manager was standing by the curtains watching the performance unfold. I pointed to the lump. "What's that?" I asked, noting that the noise emanating from the lump was increasing in volume.

"That?" said the stage manager. "that's The Creature. He's gotten lost in the curtains again; probably stoned."

"That's a person?" I asked kind of horrified. At this stage manager's nod, I walked over and unwrapped the curtains from a guy who turned out to become one of the most unlikely friends I've ever had.

Jim (not his real name either) was the son of a deceased union member. As such, he was almost automatically hired as a stage hand, if he wanted the work. Jim lived in what can only kindly be called his own world. He had been dubbed "The Creature" by the rest of the stagehands due to his belief that cutting his own hair with a scissors was a really good idea and the fact that he kept getting lost in the curtains during his assigned job as a curtain puller (his haircutting technique involved grabbing a hand full of hair on the top of his head and then lopping it off with a scissors). He lived with his mother.

I have absolutely no idea why The Creature and I hit it off. He spent a lot of time telling me tales of his dad and the old days of stage work. I took him to the few haunts I had discovered in a ratty part of Newport Beach on the California coast. One day in return, he invited me to have a drink at his favorite bar. It was the first time, he said, that he had taken anyone else there. It was a rather elaborate place featuring nude dancers. I have never been one to hang out in nude bars or strip joints, but I was a guest and we sat down at the bar. Shortly thereafter a lady came walking along top of the bar wearing a banner that said "Miss Nude Universe" and nothing else. She greeted my companion by name, warmly and with some delight. He refused at the time and thereafter to explain anything, leaving me to wonder how a guy who cut his own hair with a scissors was on a first name basis with Miss Nude Universe.

I took some ragging over my friendship with The Creature but soon enough things settled down. My acceptance by the other stagehands was confirmed one day by an incident which I was sure was going to get me fired.

Practical jokes with an edge pretty much ruled the day with our little group. During one performance about midway into my stint as a stagehand electrician, the house lights were dimmed between acts as usual. As usual also I walked out into the darkness, this time behind a prop for the Cinderella skit. I was holding the cord and plug to be inserted into a floor socket so the set would be illuminated for the dancers. All went well until I tried to insert the plug, the prongs of which had been tightly bent together.

I frantically tried to make it work. My trembling endeavor was not helped by the sound of laughter off stage. Suddenly the house lights came back up and the audience was treated to the sight of a T-shirted stagehand banging into Cinderella while sprinting for the sidelines.

The first person I ran into offstage was the Union Steward. "You dumb shit!" he said by way of greeting. But he was laughing. He was interrupted by one of the show's producers, alternately screaming in outrage and shouting that he wanted me fired. The Steward stepped forward and pointed at me. "This man is working off the Union Call Board and we stand behind him. You got a problem with that, Jack?" The producer left.

"Look, I'm really, really sorry." I started in with a full bore grovel hoping I could, at the least, receive a stay of execution. The Steward just shrugged and pointed with his chin over my shoulder. I turned around and was treated to the sight of Cinderella in her illuminated costume heading my way. I remember thinking "Well, at least I got her battery plugged in okay."

She walked up to me and gently put her hand on my cheek. "if you ever bump into me again onstage, I will cut your balls off."

I made it through to the end of the show, a total employment of about six weeks. The money was pretty good. A favorite topic of conversation before the show ended was to ask each other and discuss continually what we were going to do After. "After" was a doom filled word for most of us. After the show closed, what then? The union members were confident they could get another gig right away, so no problem. I had absolutely no idea what I would do when the show's run was over.

For weeks, The Creature had been badgering me to provide him with a copy of my resume. "Maybe I can help you get a job." I did not respond well. I mean, this guy cut his own hair and the only contact he had that I knew of was Miss Nude Universe. Finally, however, I ginned up a resume leaning heavily on my experience as a cub reporter for the Fargo (North Dakota) Forum newspaper. The resume was only a one pager but I remember it as being a fine example of my first real effort at creative writing. I gave it to The Creature on the last day of the show. We shook hands and that was it. The show's run was done.

I don't remember how long it took me to go totally broke. I do remember the day it happened. I was dangling my feet in the pool which had been a major selling point when I originally rented month-to-month lodging at the rather rundown apartment complex. I had just been informed by my landlord that I had to pay up or get out. I had already received a shut off notice for my phone and electricity; I expected them to go dark at any moment. I remember as well being totally at my wits end. I swore to God I would never go back to the Midwest and took solace in the fact I still had my van and there was a mattress in it.

The phone rang. I almost didn't answer it, but then it occurred to me that the phone company would probably not be calling to tell me they were shutting the phone off. So I ran into what for the moment was still my apartment and picked it up.

"Hello, is this Wayne?" I didn't recognize the voice. Only my friends had my phone number and this was definitely not one of them. After I responded in the affirmative, the voice went on to say "this is Art from the University of California. I have your resume here and we have a job for you right away if you're available. You can stay in the student dorm in a private room and eat at the cafeteria for free until you get settled."

And just like that, I was saved.

I later found out what had happened. The Creature took my resume that day and went to his mother's house, where he lived. He idly left it on the kitchen table. His mother, who was a public relations writer for the University of California system, thought he had left it for her. She took it to her office and presented it at the next quarterly meeting of all the PR people working for the University in case anyone needed an employee. Someone did.

From that job, everything followed. It opened the door for years of work in the media, and my own business. Through it I met the lady who was to become my wife.

I only saw The Creature one other time, about 6 months later. I had just finished dinner at a California beach restaurant called the Crab Cooker, still in business today, and there was The Creature. He was arguing with the lady at the register, trying unsuccessfully to cash a traveler's check made out to his mother, so he could pay his tab. His date was hovering nervously nearby. When she stalked out the door, I went up to my strange friend and told him I would gladly pay the bill.

He glared at me "No!" And then more softly, "No. I need to

handle this myself." He turned away and would not speak to me further.

I never ran into him again.

CHAPTER FOURTEEN

"I actually became a producer because I saw the producers getting all the babes. They were stealing them from the guitarists" Daniel Levitin.

"I'll never get sick of zombies. I just get sick of producers" George A. Romero

I never did get any babes by being a producer. That's probably because being a producer resulted from bone freezing fear and a need not to get sued.

The Day I Became an Ass Producer

Packed house. The crowd was screaming so loudly my laser operator couldn't hear me, even through his headset. He turned around to look at the audience, his mouth a perfect "O" of surprise and shock. "For God's sake, keep going!" I'm screaming now myself as I grab his arm. "Keep going, keep going!"

We were totally unqualified to stage a Star Wars, Laser Rock Show at a big Southern California amusement park. But I had a friend in the Entertainment Department there. My little company was eking out a precarious living producing corporate advertising slide shows. We hawked everything from drill bits to tar shingles, with product picture slides and a narration syncing to a soundtrack.

In one presentation we used a laser for finale effects. Now, that sort of thing is Old Hat, not done anymore. Then it was "Oh My."

Star Wars had hit. My friend saw our corporate presentation cum laser (I recall the product as being swim suits) and had a vision: Star Wars, rock and roll, lasers and finding some innocents to try and pull it off. Enter my little company.

Everything was new then, including effects lasers. Young Tech Punks had figured out that if a laser was run through optics (often consisting of such exotic materials as shower glass) weird effects could be achieved. Problem was there were only two groups of laser Tech Punks I could find. One bunch was getting rich staging nightly laser shows at the Griffith Observatory in Los Angeles. The other group was headed by a boy-genius type guy who had become a recluse after finding his new wife instead of selling medieval-style clothes at the Renaissance Faire had taken up with the Fire Eater.

I finagled a desperate meeting with the boy-genius, who heard me out impassively. "I'll help you make it work," he finally said. "That'll show the bitch." He and his team started building a set of laser optics and an operator panel.

Time was really running out. We cobbled together a soundtrack, which opened with Queen's still popular "We Will Rock You" and finished with a much cut up, disco version of the Star Wars theme.

It was during the creation of the audio track that I discovered we had a couple of problems. First, deadlines were only a vague concept for my boy-genius. Second, a subordinate in the amusement park's entertainment department felt he should have been tapped to create the show. His prophecies of doom became so strident that a significant amount of our eroding time was spent in nervous management meetings, which mostly consisted of reassurances.

Opening Day arrived. We set up and ran the sound track. The laser arrived about noon. No optics, no Boy Genius.

He and a grungy associate appeared around 2:00 PM. His cocaine-skinny colleague, Fred, nervously finger twisting his long hair, was introduced as the operator of the laser optics upon whom everything would depend during the show itself.

Thankfully everything worked great…as far as we could tell, it being a bright, sunny day which made it hard to see the laser. By 6:00 pm, with 3 hours left we were ready.

I turned to the Boy-Genius. "Well," I said cheerfully, "program the show."

"Whaddya mean," he responded. I explained that it was time for him to select and program the effects that would show up for each song. "I'm not doing that," he responded. "It's your damn show."

I eye contacted my audio guy, he shook his head no. So did everyone else except the guy who thought he should have created the show in the first place. 'Well, he can forget that shit" I thought to myself.

I walked over to a record producer friend, who seemed quite amused. "What am I going to do?" By now, I suspect "tremulous" did not cover the state of my voice control.

"You, my friend" he responded, "are now an Ass Producer. Congratulations. You are going to pull this out of your ass, and you better do it quick." He slid a chair over in front of the screen and raised his eyebrows. Well hell.

I remember we had 7 songs on the audio. The laser optic system had exactly 21 effects which worked out to 3 per song. I numbered and described each effect ("weird apple tree" etc.). My artistry consisted of picking 3 effects per song totally at random. I had the length of each song so I was able to tag how many seconds into each song different effects should appear and which effect it should be.

It was now full dark. No time for a run through. The disgruntled staff guy called it, saying "here we go, Wayne. You're screwed, you know. Curtain in 10, nine…."

"Fred!" I shouted through the headset, "you ready?"

"No!" he screamed. "I can't do this! I can't do this, I don't know what to do!"

I cursed and ran to his side with my scribbled, effects script and a stop watch in hand. My legs were shaking so badly, I'm surprised I didn't fall on him.

We had a packed house. I would shout into Fred's ear for the change of each effect and by the time we reached the finale, we could have thrown rocks at the audience and they would have shouted in appreciation.

"Artistry," raved the reviews the next day with which I was in total agreement. We played at the park for two years.

CHAPTER FIFTEEN

"What you think is going to be a big break or opportunity can sometimes turn into the opposite, and vice versa" Lydia Leonard

"Success and failure are greatly overrated. But failure gives you a whole lot more to talk about" Hildegard Knef

I honestly don't remember how we recovered from this, but recover we did. Overall, I now feel about the experience much like a guy Abraham Lincoln quoted. After the man was tarred and feathered and ridden out of town on a rail, he was asked how he liked it. He replied: "If it wasn't for the honor of the thing, I'd rather walk."

The Day We Lost Ten Grand at the Hollywood Sign.

"Well, we just tanked live in front of millions of people."

I took Gloria's hand. We hadn't been married long. This night we were sitting together at the top of Hollywood's Mt. Lee gazing down at L.A.'s evening glitter. I remember the sight as being just a notch or two short of breathtaking. I also remember thinking that this particular evening was probably not going to garner the life for us I had hoped for.

We were perched at the base of the Hollywood Sign's giant "H," the same letter from which actress Peg Entwistle had leaped to her death in 1932.

It was so damn cold. A live TV extravaganza touting the refurbished Hollywood sign, and it was actually sleeting. In southern California. And not just on the sign—and us—at the top of the mountain, but lower down too, on the stage, the TV cameras and the performers. Good thing they had a big trailer so cast and crew could warm up, outside and in. Open bar.

The Hollywood sign, originally HOLLYWOODLAND, was erected in 1923 to hawk real estate. Its projected life span was 18 months. After cinema production exploded in California, the sign was shortened to just HOLLYWOOD and became the symbol of American movies. By the 1970s the sign was a wreck. There had been a refurbishment in the 1940s, after a caretaker drunkenly drove his Model A through one of the letters, but that was pretty much it.

In 1978 Hugh Hefner threw what must have been a hell of a party at the Playboy Mansion. After it was over, he had raised just shy of a quarter million dollars for the sign's refurbishment. The City of Hollywood jumped in as did CBS. The sign's grand unveiling was to be the finale of a live, national TV special commemorating the founding of the City of Hollywood.

My office phone rang just a couple of weeks shy of the event.

"Are you the ones doing the laser thing at the park?"

We had been producing a rock and roll show at a local amusement park. It involved lasers and cheerful plagiarism of then recent rock and roll hits. It was so successful, I had actually been able to up my game to a two-room office.

When I answered in the affirmative, the caller explained that they had the contract to provide big searchlights which would illuminate the Hollywood sign at the moment of the live unveiling.

"I'm thinking," he continued, "what could be more perfect than to add lasers to the sign's unveiling? " What indeed.

Setting up lasers en plein air on top of a mountain. No power. No water; two absolute requirements. Lots of challenges but also, fame's siren call. And some money, all of which would be paid after the show aired. So it was a self-funding, big opportunity. I thought of all the zeros in my bank account and the reality of there being no numbers in front of them.

But hey! We're talking live, national television; a long walk from my small hometown in Minnesota.

Shamelessly touting CBS' involvement, I secured generators and a water truck on credit. Which left one problem: no lasers. I made screen credit promises to the laser's manufacturer, totally without authority. This secured the loan of a powerful laser. The meeting grew hostile when I then asked for two of them. The company's executives were understandably nervous. Back then, powerful Argon lasers had a glass tube of sorts which needed to be cooled by water at just the right temperature. Too hot or too cold and the tube blew up. The tubes cost $5,000.00 each.

The TV special's live entertainment was a lady named Lola Falana. I never knew her personally, but I loved the concept of her. How could you not love a woman who was a hell of a performer, had her own song (What Lola Wants, Lola Gets) and won an ownership hunk of the New York Mets baseball team in a baccarat game? Which she later sold for 14 million bucks?

She did a terrific show in the biting cold. Then came our moment. And sleet, lots of sleet.

We fired up a laser. Sleet was dripping over it. There was an immediate cracking sound as its tube blew. We frantically covered the other laser with a couple of umbrellas and hit the switch. It emanated two quick beams and blew up.

"Well," I said to Gloria the next morning. "We won't make a dime, but at least we get paid today." I called our client—the searchlight guy—thinking I'd drive over and pick up a check. The phone rang and rang. Finally, someone picked it up. "Yeah?"

I explained my plan to drive over and get paid. I heard laughter. "Good luck with that. They just declared bankruptcy."

I don't recall if I was weeping, but I had my face in my hands when Gloria shook my arm. "You have to see this." She was holding up the L.A. Times, open to a review of the show. They were raving...about us.

As it turns out, all the reporters along with cast and crew had retreated to the bar when the sleet started. They credited our company and our lasers with a beautiful illumination of the sign, actually done by the search lights of our now bankrupt employer.

It was the best review we ever got.

CHAPTER SIXTEEN

"I'm very shy really. I spend a lot of time in my room alone reading or writing or watching television" Johnny Cash

"My most brilliant achievement was my ability to be able to persuade my wife to marry me" Winston Churchill

Gloria at the time and later told me that what Cash said to her was "a lot of nonsense." I never did find out what the nonsense consisted of, and probably that's for the best.

The Day Johnny Cash Hit on My Wife

Gloria arrived from the airport. She was laughing. Her first words of "Who is that woman?" clearly indicated that something about the lady chauffer had struck a wrong note. Perhaps it was the chauffer's incessant chattering about we crew and the various, arriving Country Music luminaries. Or it could have been the Jack Boots. The chauffer had been outfitted like a lady Nazi knockoff...tight, tight grey outfit, flat, peaked hat with shiny brim; knee high black leather boots. And she was beautiful. No riding crop though, an omission duly noted by many of both genders.

I'd been up all night with my team, mostly because there wasn't enough Load In time. "Load In" is the amount of time allocated to set everything up at a performance venue. The TV cameras need "alone time" to be vectored in, the sound crew needs time and silence to do their work and so on. This undoubtedly had contributed to a hell of a fist fight in center stage around 2:00 AM the previous night. The combatants were the head of the lighting crew and the boss of the sound team.

The pending broadcast, a Country Music TV special, would cover a third of the country live; tape delay for everyone else. We all felt we had hunks of our careers on the line; no one was giving an inch. There had been a lot of shouting.

We were in Tulsa Oklahoma. This all took place before the advent of the small, powerful computers currently used to control special effects on stage shows. Now you can even buy such computers off the shelf, ready for use.

Then, for us to provide unusual visuals and pictures as part of a live "for TV" concert, we had to cobble together some 30 slide projectors and a couple of lasers by hand. "Slide projectors"—which pretty much exist no more—were about the only way to project bright still images and pictures onto a large screen. Boxy, mechanical devices, each weighing a few pounds, a single slide projector could be loaded with about 80 images. Now, one smart phone weighing a few ounces can project many hundreds of images. Now is better. Much better.

Getting our dozens of mechanical projectors and two lasers to work in tandem, much less work at all, was the embodiment of tying up marbles with a piece of string. It took hours to align everything. We were given 45 minutes to get ready. And we were first up. The opening, God help us.

Well before sun up, the Country Music impresario who was staging the event had finally blown in from the street. And he was really, really pissed, probably at himself as much as anyone else for hiring a famous singing family to stage the event with their new production company. It was their first production. As it turned out, their previous staging work, aside from singing hits, had apparently been a bit inflated during the sales process.

The Impresario lined us up, pointedly ignoring the battered

faces of two of his critical team. He then allocated blocks of time to each crew. The assigned set up times would end a couple of hours before the show started, so in theory all would be ready. Problem was, no individual block of time was sufficient to complete all the work each team had to do.

"Well," opined my crew chief, "if we just bag this, we know we'll fail. If we give it a go, we'll almost certainly fail, but it will be spectacular." Our all-night-without-sleep strategy was to blow off our finale fireworks to start instead of to end our segment. Following that, we'd try to align the 3 dozen pieces of projection equipment on the fly, as they ran in front of live TV cameras. "Well, hell," I thought, "what could possibly go wrong with that?"

By mid-morning everything for us was as ready as it would get.

The show was due to run later that day. After spinning a pack of lies about Tulsa, I had previously convinced my wife Gloria to interrupt her Ph.D. studies and fly in for the show. As she hadn't arrived just yet, I and my crew chief, Jerry, took a break to walk around the building. Joining Jerry and I was a guy who had been asking incessant questions about our set up. All night he had been watching us closely while clasping a bowling bag. Blue plastic. Ersatz Mother of Pearl handles. A bowling bag. He never let go of it.

"What's with the stupid bag?" I asked, politely I thought, as we ambled along. He stopped. I thought at first he was going to hit me with the damn thing. Instead, he cracked it open. It was completely stuffed with money, lots and lots of money. He explained that he was road manager for a singer who was trying to transition to the Country Music genre. They hoped to bump into Johnny Cash at some point during the show. The singer was one whose previous work and music I loved and who was later inducted into the Rock and Roll Hall of Fame. "He likes walking around money." Jerry and I looked at the money, then at each other. No one said anything.

Show time. The red "we're live" light blinked and we hit the pyros, which were supposed to end our segment, not start it. What saved us is that they went off; loud cracks! and lots of smoke. We rolled the lasers through the smoke, which to my grateful surprise, looked pretty cool. Then, standing on scaffolds, our small team frantically tried to hand align the multitude of slide projectors, all unstoppably cycling through differing images and parts of images. Our desperate procedure was to grab various projectors and try to match up their constantly changing images with whatever popped up from other projectors. All of this was directed onto a huge screen; the whole mess barfing out onto live TV. My last memory of that effort was the two sides of the face of a much-loved lady Country singer, hopping across the screen until they came together with her nose landing at her hairline.

Jumping down, I bumped into my acquaintance with the bowling bag. "That was really...something," he said and steered us to the backstage bar. Gloria had passed on the bar, staying instead in the stage wings to watch the show. When I emerged from the bar, I couldn't see her. What I could see was a big crowd of entertainers and crew alike all standing in a group, watching something. Watching something in respectful silence. I climbed back up on the scaffold to see what was up. There, standing in the middle of a huge circle of people was a tall guy in a black shirt...and Gloria.

By the time I got back down the crowd had dissipated. I walked up to Gloria. "What did he say?" I asked.

"A lot of nonsense," she answered smiling. "He said 'Little Lady' a lot," a big mistake then and now.

"Do you know who that was?" I asked. She shook her head in the negative. "Johnny Cash," I said.

She blinked. "Who's Johnny Cash?"

We went home later that day.

I don't know if the singer and his road manager with all the walking around money ever connected with Johnny Cash. But I do know that shortly after the events in Tulsa, their touring plane, burning from fuselage to tail, smashed through a line of trees and bellied into a Texas cow pasture. They were just two miles short of the runway. All aboard died except the pilot and co-pilot who, badly burned, crawled out of the cockpit windows. The entertainer in back, his lady, his band and his bowling bag road manager, died. At the time it was widely rumored that freebasing cocaine caused the fire. The NTSB (National Transportation Safety Board) refuted this, saying the likely cause was a faulty cabin heater.

I happened to be with Jerry, my Tulsa crew chief, when we got the news.

"Dark side of the force," was his only comment.

CHAPTER SEVENTEEN

"You have to play defense, that's how you win" Peter Bondra

"Age is getting to know all the ways the world turns, so that if you cannot turn the world the way you want, you can at least, get out of the way so you won't get run over" Miriam Makeba

There's been a lot written about how brutal things can be in the entertainment industry. I thought so too at the time. Later, it became apparent that there's nothing like running your own business to really have sharks chew on your leg. Just because they can.

The Day We Triggered The Doomsday Code

I had already been broke enough times to recognize desperation when I saw it in another vendor. The electrician seemed like a nice enough guy, a family man if the baby shoes hanging from his truck's mirror were any indication.

I was meeting with the owner of a manufacturing company for whom we were writing a software program. The electrician had come by at the owner's invitation to pick up a check for previously completed work. I could tell the electrician really needed the money. And so, apparently, could the guy who owed it to him.

"Your check is ready," said the owner to the electrician's great and obvious relief. "I've just got a couple of things for you to take a look at and I'll give it to you." The electrician blinked in surprise. "But, I did all the other work, and you told me to come by and get my check."

"LISTEN!" the owner got red faced. "I've got your Goddamned check! I just need you to look at a couple of things and I'll give it to you!" The electrician stood in silence for a few moments. A variety of emotions chased across his face, the "I gotta get paid today. I don't dare piss this guy off" one clearly leading the pack.

I had a lengthy meeting with the owner; it didn't wrap up until a couple of hours later. As I was leaving, the electrician came back to the door. "I took care of everything; it was just a bit over two hours of extra work I'll need to bill you for."

"WHAT?" The owner stood up from his desk. "I told you to just look at some stuff. If you did more work that's YOUR friggin' problem; I won't pay one more damn penny. Speaking of which, you screwed around so long, my book keeper left. You'll need to come back for your check; call me in a couple of days and we'll set it up. Or I can mail it."

I didn't see what happened in the office after that, but as I was getting into my car the electrician came out cursing, clearly checkless.

When you're a small business person, you run into a lot of bad stuff, most of it involving getting paid. One of the worst is known as "Chasing Your Money." You have a contract. You do the work. It's time to be paid. Then there's "just one more thing," or "other things to check" and pretty soon you've done a lot of extra work for free just to get paid for the first round of stuff you've already done. The smaller or more desperate you are, the more likely it is you'll be treated to this sort of thing. And if you simply can't afford delays in payment or going to court, there's no real recourse except to smile grimly and take the hammering.

A bunch of years ago, my wife and I founded and ran a small, custom software development company. She did the work, I made the sales. At the time there was no Google, really, as we know it today; no App Store, no free software or software you could simply subscribe to in your area of need and access on line for a few bucks a month.

Then, if you wanted software, pretty much someone had to create it just for you, which is where we came in. Software at that time didn't "live" in the cloud or on remote servers so you could just log in and use or download it. Software then, when completed, had to be installed by the developer directly into a buyer's computers.

This left developers like us really exposed. To get paid, you had to essentially turn over your product to the customer in full working order. Once installed in a customer's computers, it could then be copied, including all its code, in an instant. Effectively then, there was nothing to repossess in the event of non-payment. Even if you could repossess your software program and it hadn't been copied, the work was created for the needs of one particular client and therefore was pretty much unsellable to anyone else.

To protect ourselves, we had adopted a system of "pay as you go" billings in our contracts. There was no option, however, to having the last payment due upon completion of work, the installation of our custom developed software into our customer's computers and a demonstration that it worked as ordered. So, inescapably, as we got to our last payment, our client would have our product installed, completely usable, and able to be copied with a few keystrokes. And the last payment was where the vast majority of our profit resided.

To solve this "last payment" dilemma as best we could, our contracts were crystal clear that our last payment was absolutely, positively due the day of installation of our software, and before the actual installation itself. We always confirmed that the last payment check was ready and would be given to us when we arrived for the installation. We had completed dozens of programs and thus far had not had any final payment problems.

But after watching our current client's treatment of another vendor, I had a really bad feeling about this one.

I met with the rest of the team; my wife Gloria, who

interviewed clients and designed the database and my brother Dave, who wrote the software code. I outlined what had happened and my assessment that we were involved with a bad guy. I absolutely did not know how to protect us, but my little voice was shouting that we'd better come up with something.

Silence fell, finally broken by Gloria. "Doomsday Code" she said.

I was mystified. "What?"

She turned to Dave. "Can you program in four passwords? One which can always open the program, which we'll give him if he pays us as called for in our contract. If he doesn't pay, we open the program with a different password, which will trigger our Doomsday Code. I want the Doomsday Code to require a new password every 10 days for a month following the trigger. Can you do that?

Dave started laughing. "Piece of cake."

True to his word, Dave programmed in the password "Open," which would always open the software. Then, he programmed in a password of "Bunt" (Latin for Doomsday). If the password "Bunt" was typed in when we installed the software instead of "Open", the requirement of the software needing new passwords as time went by would be triggered. Ten days after entering the password "Bunt," the software would demand a different password or it would not open. The second password was "Impetus" (Latin for attack). Ten days after "Impetus" was typed in, the software would demand yet another password, which Dave programmed in as "Culus" (Latin for asshole). This final password would forever afterwards be the password needed to open the software.

Delivery day arrived. The client confirmed our check was ready and that he would turn it over when we arrived to do the installation, just as called for in our contract.

We arrived for installation. I asked for our check. He glared at me. "I'll give you your check when you've installed the software. Otherwise, I'm paying you for nothing." We'd had this happen once or twice before, and all had worked out fine.

"O.K.," I said, and we installed the software. The opening screen came up, demanding a password.

"What's the password?" our client asked. I reminded him we were now to be given our check. He got right into my face, an inch away. "LISTEN TO ME, YOU JERK," he screamed. "YOU'D BETTER GIVE ME THE PASSWORD, AND RIGHT NOW!"

He slammed himself down at the computer. "Now what's the Goddamned password?" We stared at each other.

"Bunt," I told him. And he typed it in.

The software opened right up and I asked for our check again. "I'll give it to you after we've gone through everything, and my staff is trained," he responded. We went through the whole program with his staff, which was part of our normal procedure anyway. Everything worked just fine, and the staff, I recall, were delighted at the potential of using it.

It was now almost 5:00 PM. We were finished. I asked for our check. "I've been thinking about that," he said with a smile, which I remember thinking looked a bit smug. "Everything seems to work O.K., but I want to use it for a couple of days just to be sure."

I reminded him of our contract terms and that I needed to be paid. He started shouting again. "Get the hell out of here! You can pick up your check day after tomorrow!"

We left. Two days later I was told he decided he'd mail the check that day, so I didn't need to come by personally. By the end of the next week, no check had arrived, but 10 days had elapsed. The phone rang.

"The program says we need a different password," said our client. "What is it?" I responded that we had not gotten our check and we had to be paid.

"You Sonavabitch!" he screamed into the phone. "I'll send your check tonight! NOW WHAT'S THE PASSWORD?"

I asked him to give me his word he'd send our payment that day. "Yes, YES! You have my word! NOW WHAT'S THE PASSWORD?" Then there was mention of a lawsuit.

"Type in 'Impetus,'" I told him. After a pause, "That worked," he said. "Lucky for you."

Another 10 days elapsed. No check. The phone rang. This time, he actually seemed a bit subdued. "I need another password."

"No surprise there," I answered. "We never got our check."

"You can come on by tomorrow and pick it up," he responded.

"No," I answered, "I won't need to."

"You won't?"

"Nope. Because you're going to wire us our final payment in full, tomorrow morning. Then I give you the last password."

I hung up shortly thereafter, feeling that I wasn't getting paid enough to listen to a final round of threats and screaming. We got our money in the morning and he got his password. We made our Doomsday Code a standard feature from then on, but we never had to trigger it with anyone else. Most people really are pretty honest.

A year later I was told our Doomsday client had filed for bankruptcy, buried under a mountain of lawsuits and Small Claims Court judgments. I never did hear if the electrician with the baby shoes on his mirror ever got his money. But thankfully we did get ours.

CHAPTER EIGHTEEN

"Take life with a grain of salt...a slice of lime, and a shot of tequila"
Author Unknown

I wouldn't trade growing up in a small mid-west town, especially the fishing part. The only problem with it, is that if you leave you can find your notion of people and How Things Work just ain't necessarily so.

The Day They Tried to Kill Us in Arkansas

It was 1966. We were young. We were immortal.

And for that we almost got ourselves murdered one night in Arkansas.

We were four fraternity brothers at a small Minnesota College. We decided that our spring break would be best spent driving from Minnesota to New Orleans, where the drinking age was low and much winked at, there were parties everywhere, and it was warm. Or so we believed, and that was enough.

It was 1966, square in the middle of a decade of enormous civil rights turmoil. None of us were political in the slightest. Even had we been so, a cursory check would have shown that the Freedom Rider campaign had ended in 1961 (the Freedom Rider campaign had involved a lot of volunteers, some of them young and white, heading into the deep South to register black voters. That campaign was revived a few years later as Freedom Summer).

Four young black children were killed when their church in Birmingham, Alabama, was bombed in 1963. That same year, Commissioner of Public Safety there, "Bull" Connor released his dogs on protesters and their families, including a lot of little kids.

In 1964, Mississippi Klansmen, with the deep involvement of local law enforcement, murdered three civil rights workers about our age and buried them in a dirt levy.

The landmark voting rights bill had become law in 1965. That same year, just a few months before we planned our New Orleans spring break, Viola Liuzzo, a young, white civil rights worker from Michigan, had her brains blown out in Alabama. The perpetrators were four Klansmen who pulled alongside her on a public highway in broad daylight outside of Montgomery and repeatedly fired through her side car window. Her offense was primarily that of having a young, black man in the car with her.

There was more, but we were oblivious to all of it. And truth be told, had we known, it would have had no traction; we would've still headed out. In the little Minnesota town where I grew up and our college was located, civil rights issues were far away and viewed with some perplexity. Besides, it was now 1966 and all that stuff was ancient history.

We took my car, a much loved (by me, anyway) bottle green, old Oldsmobile four-door sedan. There were two reasons for this: first it was a big old boat of a car with plenty of room for the four of us. Second I was the only one who had a car.

I don't remember what luggage we took except that a major part of it part of it was multiple cases of really bad beer. Our clothes we jammed in the trunk; the beer traveled in a place of honor between whichever two passengers were in the backseat. We stopped only for gas and occasional fast food. We didn't want to waste a minute of our imagined spring break delights in New Orleans, so our driving was in shifts, nonstop.

On either the first or second day of our drive, 2:00 AM found us alone on the highway, as far as we could tell anyway, somewhere in deep Arkansas. I was in back, having just completed my driving shift. I was now happily seated alongside the beer and my pal Mike, who at that time was president of our Fraternity. There were two Mikes in our group. One of them was seated beside me in the back of the car; the other was driving.

A car pulled up behind us.

There were no red police lights nor was there any siren. But there were two intense spotlights that pierced into our back window. We pulled over and stopped. They pulled over and stopped. We all sat there for a few minutes. We rolled down the side windows so we could hear any orders emanating from behind us. Nothing. We still felt it was police that had pulled us over. And perhaps it was, even though there were no "police lights" or other police-type car identifiers we were used to in Minnesota. After many minutes of nothing happening we decided to slowly pull away.

The instant our car moved, the back window blew inward. I heard the Mike who was sitting beside me cry "Owwww!" and something slammed into my face. Yep, I had just been shot, although I didn't figure that out until later.

I think it knocked me a little loopy. I remember shouting that deathless phrase: "They got me!" an exclamation I find embarrassing to this very day, it being not exactly a romantic, manly utterance in a time of danger.

The next thing I recall was looking across our cases of beer to my backseat partner Mike. He was cursing, loudly and creatively, and had blood streaming from his cheek where a bullet had given him something resembling a saber cut. Blood was pouring off my own chin, and I felt around to see what was intact. I quickly discovered that I had indeed been shot... in the nose.

I looked out through the space where the back window had been. I could see the other car still a bit back as we had apparently, with a complete lack of planning, gotten the jump on them. Little pinpricks of light were emanating from each side of the following car. "Now that's kind of weird," I thought. Then I realized they were shooting at us. And they were gaining.

The other Mike, who was driving, had my old jalopy cranked up to its max speed, but we were steadily losing the most important race of our lives. Rich, the fourth member of our quartet, with a calm that must have served him well during his later fighter pilot career in the Marine Corps, was leaning back in the front seat against the doorjamb which put him sort of out of the line of fire, luckily for all of us as it turned out. He was quietly giving ongoing advice to driver Mike as to how to take curves at high speed. Rich was also the one who spotted our salvation: the exit for Waldron, Arkansas.

We careened onto it and the other car did not follow. Now here's a question—when you are four young guys raised in Minnesota and you've just been shot up what's the first thing you do? Easy answer: you go to the police. Which is what we did.

A long while after our frantic phone call, a guy showed up who was at least wearing some kind of uniform, a comfort of sorts. His reaction was not what I expected. "Well now," he said as he walked around my car checking out the bullet holes, "Well now."

We were all standing outside of the police station, which was totally dark and empty. I believe the police contingent in Waldron, Arkansas was and probably is yet today quite small. As nearly as I can determine from my research, Waldron's population at that time was well under 2000 people. By now it was probably around 4:00 AM or so and still dark. Our emergency responder invited us inside the police station. As we trooped in, I noticed the building also had multiple cells in back, each empty with its door open. The building apparently did double duty as both the police station and the town jail.

He made a phone call. His first words were "I got some boys here who've been shot up, nothing serious." I started mentally grousing that "nothing serious" depended on which side of the "shot up" thing you were on. After his opening line, his end of the conversation consisted of grunts and things like "yeah?" and "uh huh."

He hung up the phone. Then he put his hand on his gun, kicked me, and ordered us all into one of the cells (I cannot tell you why he picked me as the one to kick). The doomish clang of the cell door was followed by utter silence. We stared at each other. Not one of us could think of a word to say.

Now I don't know who was called that night. But I do know that Sallisaw, Oklahoma, was and is about an hour's drive up the road from Waldron, Arkansas. It's also across a state line, convenient if you live in Waldron and have a sudden urge to split some out of state fried chicken with a Sallisaw counterpart. Alternately, if you needed a helping hand with making some pesky Arkansas situation disappear into a jurisdiction in another state, relief was just a phone call and an hour's drive away. At that time, I'm told, Sallisaw, Oklahoma was not a whole lot bigger than Waldron, Arkansas, both being small towns in rural, Southern communities.

The sun came up and office staff appeared. We were informed that we were being extradited to Sallisaw Oklahoma and there were some papers to sign. I don't recall them threatening us over that, but they really didn't have to--we were just four shot-up college kids, scared half to death. At least two of us were underage as well, so whatever was signed really couldn't be enforced. But I suppose it was important to observe the proprieties. I asked to make a phone call and laughter ensued. No phone call.

We were in Sallisaw, Oklahoma before noon that same day, locked up in yet another jail. Shot and two jails in less than 24 hours. The wheels of justice did not grind slowly for us.

John Steinbeck described his Okie characters (the Joads) in Grapes of Wrath, as being refugees from the fair city of Sallisaw. The trek from their home in Sallisaw Oklahoma to California was the lynch pin around which the novel spins its sad tale. The term "Okie" became part of the national lexicon, thanks to Grapes of Wrath. Sallisaw is at the end of the Trail of Tears, the death filled march of mostly Cherokee Indians assaulted at gunpoint and robbed of their possessions and homes east of the Mississippi, as part of then national policy.

Sallisaw's real claim to fame, however, is a Favorite Son named

Pretty Boy Floyd. Pretty Boy became a famous criminal during the depression of the 1930s, mostly by robbing banks. In the end, he was beloved, as it was said he would tear up farmers' mortgage papers during the course of his bank heists. He was killed in 1934, shot to death in an Ohio cornfield. It is estimated between 20,000 and 40,000 people attended Pretty Boy Floyd's funeral just outside of Sallisaw. It was and remains the largest funeral ever held in Oklahoma.

Pretty Boy's brother, EW Floyd, apparently decided to follow the dictum of the old saw "If you can't beat 'em, join em." Riding, I'm sure, on considerable name recognition, EW got himself elected as sheriff of Sallisaw twice. The last time was in 1955, following a short hiatus after an election loss to a gentleman by the name of Huckleberry Shell. EW hung on to his position thereafter like a barnacle from his 1955 re-election as Sherriff until his death in 1970.

So, when we were so quickly moved from a jail in Waldron, Arkansas to a jail in Sallisaw, Oklahoma, it was during the law-enforcement reign in Sallisaw of bank robber Pretty Boy Floyd's brother, Sheriff EW Floyd.

Now, to be completely clear, in all the records I can find there's not a whisper of scandal in EW's tenure as sheriff of Sallisaw, Oklahoma. Also, I have absolutely no knowledge of or any evidence at all that the person our responder in Waldron Arkansas called or subsequently made some kind of deal with was Sallisaw Sherriff EW Floyd, although in retrospect it all seems pretty convenient. I will say that if you're into reading between the lines, in the middle of EW's tenure, in 1960 a huge 105-acre racetrack was approved and set up just outside of Sallisaw, which was still quite a small town. Seems a little strange.

The "jail" in Sallisaw was actually just a huge concrete room. There were metal cages in the center of the room up on blocks, each "cage" containing six, fold-down bunks. The "cages" were locked during the day, to be opened up for eight hours only each night as a sleep aid for the unwilling guests of Sallisaw's law enforcement. Other than those eight hours, everyone just sat around on the cold and filthy concrete floor, there being no chairs or furniture at all.

At one end of the huge room was a high window letting in a bit of light from the outside. At the other was a single toilet fully open to view by everyone and the source of many catcalls when being used by new arrivals. Above the toilet was a huge and rather spectacular, detailed drawing of a man/woman oral sex act. I was mystified the entire time we were there as to where the drawing materials had come from, as we weren't allowed even a toothbrush.

The room was almost empty when we were put into it, a huge door clanging shut behind us. We later found out that our early morning arrival was unusual. Most new guests in the Sallisaw jail back then arrived in the late afternoon or early evening, we later discovered. Sentences and court dates were seemingly timed so that large numbers of inmates would ebb and flow in the late afternoon and early evening, thereby, I suspect, saving the city the cost of at least two meals per inmate.

The facility we were in as it turned out was generally not for the housing of long-term prisoners, so we were greeted by only two other souls that first morning of our stay in the Sallisaw jail. One of them was, he claimed, a rodeo cowboy about our own age. He maintained that he had just gotten 30 days in the Sallisaw slammer for busting up a bar and then not having any money to pay for damages (apparently the winnings from his rodeo career were a bit sparse). The other was an older guy, probably around 50 or so, which by today's reckoning is pretty young. He was a rather frequent guest due to a serious and ongoing love for large volumes of alcohol.

Meeting those two was a whole lot of good luck after a spectacularly bad run. The Cowboy took us under his wing, deciding for reasons of his own to keep us physically intact and to pass along his hard-earned experience in jail protocol. The Old Man decided he liked us as well and stuck close, becoming an ongoing source of gossip about the jail staff and every new miscreant that was thrown into our concrete room. Our blood-spattered appearance gave them both an excuse to initiate conversation when we first appeared, although it was clear our story was viewed with considerable skepticism.

The Cowboy was stuck in the Sallisaw jail for another four weeks or so. The Old Man did not want to leave as he had no place else to go, he said, and it was still cold in Oklahoma. He threatened to hit (or stab) anyone who tried to take him out of the cell. As far as I could tell, everyone from the Sheriff on down pretty much left the Old Man alone.

As our first Sallisaw day wore on, more men started being added into the room, many of them pretty rough looking and absolutely not the type you would want to invite home to meet the family. The Old Man, rather delightedly I thought, informed us that one of our new arrivals had been picked up on suspicion of murder while another had a long, thin knife stuck down the inside of one boot. I never did discover if any of this was true, but I did give more credence to the knife rumor as the frisking procedure in the Sallisaw jail left a lot to be desired, which is to say there was no procedure at all.

9 o'clock was the magic hour for the opening of the cages and our 8-hour access to bunks and their thin mattresses. Shortly before this much-anticipated moment, the Cowboy and the Old Man took us aside.

"Now listen," said the Cowboy, "This is really serious. There's six of us and there are six bunks in each cage. When they open them up we go to the last one in line and no one else gets in. No one. Believe me, you do not want that to happen. We fight if we have to. We fight. And remember, whatever it takes, nobody else gets in but the six of us."

The 9 o'clock hour arrived. The jailer actually had a big ring of jangling keys, like a prop from an old black-and-white movie. "Okay animals," he said cheerfully as he unlocked doors. "Time to go to bed!"

We piled into the last cage in the row. The Cowboy and the Old

Man were the front-line contingent of our little band. They stood in front of the door with us four behind. The Old Man was shaking.

The Cowboy looked back at us. "Get ready," he said.

Then he looked out at the milling crowd. "We are full up here" was all he said. But he said it loudly, with a level stare. The crowd looked at us for a heartbeat. Two. Then they all turned aside and filed into the other open doors. And that's the way it worked for the rest of the time we were in the Sallisaw jail. As we laid down on our chosen bunks that evening and the lights dimmed, the Cowboy added a last instruction. "One other thing," he said. "No matter what you hear tonight, leave it alone. You understand me? Whatever you hear, just leave it alone." I remember sleeping well that first night and I don't recall hearing anything at all.

I made a request every day to be allowed to make a phone call. And every day I was refused. One time the official to whom I made my plea, just smiled a bit and said "you thought you would come down here and help the ni***rs. Well, welcome to Oklahoma."

The days passed. The Cowboy tended to be morose for hours at a stretch, just sitting on the floor, so when I wasn't talking with my friends I struck up conversations with the Old Man. Conversations with him were a spotty affair. He often broke into a ditty, mid-sentence: "What's the word? Thunderbird. What's the price? 50 twice." (Thunderbird, was a very bad, very cheap wine which I believe is no longer made).

One day I noticed he had been gone for an extended period so I wandered around looking for him. I found the Old Man standing underneath the one window in our jail. He was fiddling with a tin can, which he immediately stuck back up on the windowsill when he saw me approach. "It's just Pruno," he said a little desperately. "Please don't tell anyone." Pruno, I later found out, is the name for homemade prison wine, if wine it can be called. The formula depends on materials at hand; generally, fruit juice, and bits of fruit or vegetables. Then you add in a little bread for the yeast and finish it off with sunshine and a lot of optimism.

"You want to try it?" he asked hopefully. I acquiesced and took a slug. They say you never forget your first date or your first drag on a cigarette. I will never forget my first and last taste of the Old Man's Pruno. It was awful beyond my powers of description.

In the end, it was the Old Man who unwittingly provided us the means to get out of jail. During our conversations, he had given me the name of the sheriff and the names of all the trustees and the other officials who kept turning down my requests for a phone call. One day he sought me out and pointed to a new deputy who was delivering what passed for breakfast. The Old Man then told me the person's name, and suggested I "lay my con on him" since he knew I had been trying to get a phone call out. I can only attribute that wonderful advice to the Old Man and my's bonding over Pruno.

I walked up to the new guy. "Hey (whatever his name was, as I have now completely forgotten), EW said that when you came on, you would take me down so I can make a phone call."

"That right?"

Lying my ass off, I assured him that I had just repeated the gospel according to Sheriff EW Floyd, at which point he took me by the arm. He was a big guy. "O.K. I'm not going to cuff you. If you give me any trouble I'm going to beat the shit out of you."

My mother was fortunately at home to take the call, which naturally had to be a collect call. She was frantic; it had been many days since anyone had heard from us. I interrupted her string of borderline angry questions to ask her if she had a pencil handy. She did and I cheerfully gave her the name of the sheriff, the town, and the direct phone number for the jail, which I could read off the (as we now consider it) old-fashioned dial phone, the type that used to have the phone number under a piece of plastic in the middle of the dial. So far so good.

I then breathlessly told her as fast as I could that we had been shot and were in deep trouble. My new friend slammed down the phone and frog marched me back to the cell. For those of you who don't know what that is, a "frog march" is when a strong someone grabs your collar and the back of your pants, lifting your pants up as high as possible. They then push you forward causing you to tiptoe ahead with your pants and underwear uncomfortably jammed up between your buttocks. It is possible to resist this, but it is difficult in the best of circumstances; more so when the person behind you has a gun.

When I was bodily thrown back into the cell, the Old Man looked up. "How did it go?" he asked.

I told him it went very well. Actually, it went a whole lot better than very well, how much better I only found out later.

The general of the whole operation was my mother. Really, EW never stood a chance.

We are talking here about a woman who until the day she died denied any involvement with "Presley for President" being painted in huge letters on a water tower a few blocks from our house, causing great uproar in both the civil and religious communities in Moorhead, Minnesota. She also always maintained it was sheer coincidence that she had boxes of "Presley for President" buttons available the next day for promotional giveaway at the record store she owned.

After our conversation, she had immediately made three phone calls and I don't know in what order. One call was to the president of the college I was attending, whose name was John Neumaier. Another call was to our local newspaper, where I had worked as a cub reporter. The third call was to a person reputed to be the best lawyer in town.

I was later told by a local Sallisaw lawyer that almost instantly after my call, the phone in the Sallisaw jail started ringing. I will hand it to EW and his team, they fought a strong rearguard action.

They initially told the newspaper that we had had a gun battle with police, which only heightened the frenzy. Then they told our lawyer that we had threatened people with a knife, which was later and quickly changed to a beer bottle as they could find no knives in our car. But I will admit they probably found a lot of beer bottles.

Total capitulation took place when calls were received at the jail within minutes inquiring about our health, first from the rather renowned president of our college and then directly and personally from the Governor of Minnesota. It seems our college president was personal friends with the Governor and had used that friendship to get the Governor to call, taking a huge gamble that we really were just four college kids in big trouble and not a carload of criminals.

It wasn't 20 minutes after my phone call that EW himself showed up. He was flanked by a couple of deputies as he walked into the cell block. He looked us over and then glared at his deputies. "Why, these boys have been hurt. Get them down to the hospital right now so they can be checked out."

And off we went. I even got a candy bar out of the deal from the hospital vending machine. It was far too late for stitches. Fortunately, our wounds were minor and no one had gotten glass in their eyes. We did not see EW Floyd again.

Our lawyer and my Father showed up as fast as transportation would allow. My Father's and my adult relationship began when my Father looked at me, surveyed my blood splattered shirt and said, "someone is going to pay for this" and it was clear he didn't mean me.

We were all told that in the spirit of cooperation, a hearing would be held immediately so everyone could figure out what steps should be taken going forward. The moment of the hearing arrived and we were ushered into a small, extremely littered office. Other than all of us, there were only two people present. One was a lady sitting behind an old wooden desk and the other was a tall skinny guy hopping from one foot to the other. Turns out the Hopper was a local attorney. We were never introduced to either of them nor informed as to what their roles were in the whole affair.

Our lawyer started in gamely enough. "We would like to work with you so that hearings or whatever you require can be scheduled around these boys' education."

"Well," responded the lady behind the desk, "Why don't you just give me a call with what you want to do?"

At this rather laid-back approach to the law, our attorney's mouth opened and closed a few times. He finally got out "Ah, well, this is pretty serious. How about the week right after Easter? They have a break then."

"That's really a bad time for me," the lady responded. "My daughter comes home then and all."

By now the local attorney had become very agitated. He took us out in the hall and stared at our lawyer. "Will you people please just get the hell out of here? Your car is downstairs. Just go. Now. You'll never hear anything more about this, and there'll be no record, I guarantee it. You can be hundreds of miles away by evening" making clear, I thought, that we should not hang around until dark.

So we left. We were hungry, it now being lunch time. A local restaurant refused to serve us when staff asked, "were you the ones in jail?" and were answered in the affirmative. A few miles down the road we found both anonymity and lunch. Less than 48 hours later, we were back home, sleeping in our own beds.

Spring break was over a week or so later. I remember being depressed when I arrived back on campus. Actually, I thought I was going kind of crazy. We had only known the Cowboy and the Old Man for a few days, and I found myself wondering continually how they were doing with the four of us gone and empty bunks to fill in their Sallisaw cage. We never even had a chance to say adios. Or thanks for that matter. The Old Man concerned me in particular, with his God-awful Pruno and his ditty and his gossip about people being arrested for murder or having knives down their boot. Stupid old guy. I couldn't stop thinking about how he shook with fear when we all stood in the door of the cage. But he didn't move.

Adding to my distress, I looked like a Ronald McDonald wannabe. That bullet that grazed Mike on the cheek left him with what could pass as a dueling scar. He was a handsome bastard to begin with and was now only more so. My hit, which went through my nose, left me with a bulbous gauze bandage, strongly resembling the ball-like nose of a clown.

"Hey Wayne!" Three young ladies from our "sister sorority" had spotted me and were angling across the hub of the campus. One of them was a lady whom, truth to tell, I had had my eye on for some time. "Oh boy," I thought. "Here it comes. Mockery and clown comments."

They walked up. The person I found of most interest eyed me speculatively. "Does your car really have a lot of bullet holes in it? Can we see it?"

They looked it over, uttering many awed noises. Then I was asked if it still ran. When I answered yes, I received an immediate offer of free drinks that afternoon. My contribution was to be to provide a ride in the riddled car with a stop at the sorority house to show others and to pick up a few more players for an afternoon of hooky at a local bar.

My car full of ladies...and me. All right! I kept that car for a long, long time. I never filled in the bullet holes, but I did sand them occasionally so they always looked new.

In the weeks following our adventure, I found myself being nagged by a couple of things. One was being wrenched out of sleep occasionally by the remembered "bang!" of my car's back window exploding and the sight of muzzle flashes from the car behind us, all thankfully fading away as wakefulness ensued. The other was a question my mind just kept niggling at regarding our escape from what I now believe was a very dangerous situation.

My occasional insomnia disappeared but the nagging question did not so I asked for and received a short meeting with the much-liked president of our college, Dr. John Neumaier, who students respectfully called "The Doc" (they also called the final construction work done on campus "Neumaier's Last Erection, respect being a relative thing with college students). His personal intercession with our jailers and the enlisting of his friend, Karl Rolvaag, the Governor of Minnesota to do this same, undoubtedly was the primary cause of our being disgorged from durance vile, and probably saved us from much worse than just being lightly wounded.

He was seated at his desk as I entered. We shook hands briefly.

"And what can I do for you, young man?" He asked.

Thanking him for his time, I replied that I had a question to ask that had really been bothering me.

He looked over. "Yes?"

It just burst out of me. "Why did you do it? What if we really had been guilty of something?" I now will shamefully admit that I expected something banal in response like "I got to know you when you dated my daughter a couple of times" or "you all seemed like fine young men."

Instead he stood up and walked over to the window, gazing out at a dreary, rain filled Minnesota day. Then he started to talk.

He spoke of Krystalnacht, of the Nazis murdering his mother, the First Contralto in the Frankfurt Opera. Of the state sponsored murders of his many uncles, cousins and friends.

"After I escaped in 1939 I swore to myself that I would never, never, NEVER stand by!" At each "never" his fist banged down on the windowsill.

Tears were streaming down his face when he turned away from the window. To my surprise, moisture was tracking down my own cheeks as well. I found I couldn't speak, so we shook hands once more and I left in silence.

I will say that things were never the same for me after that. Life assumptions nurtured from childhood in a safe, white bread, small Minnesota town, ever after tangled with the visceral knowledge that there really are bad, bad folks out there. People who do terrible things and not only feel good about it but are elevated in stature in their communities for having done so.

I have tried to do the best I can with my life and I don't have too many regrets, not really. One I do have, which will stay with me until the end, is that before he died I never told The Doc how I came to realize what an enormous act of courage it was, what he did. To not only put his own professional and personal neck on the line, to risk it all for four college kids he really didn't know, but to put into play a personal friendship and what must've been enormous political capital. He got the Governor of Minnesota to pick up the phone and call that little jail in Oklahoma. "We know you have those four boys down there and nothing had better happen to them."

I think John Neumaier saved our lives.

Dr. John J. Neumaier passed away on May 30, 2016 at the age of 94. Former Minnesota Governor, Karl Rolvaag, died in December 1990. Mike, my also shot seatmate, served in Vietnam and later built a prosperous career as an engineer and in real estate. The other Mike, who was driving that night, became a successful dentist and Rich made a career as a Marine Corps fighter pilot. With his wife, he spends summers on their mid-western farm and winters on a boat in the Caribbean.

As predicted, as soon as we were gone, the record of our being shot in Arkansas and locked up in Oklahoma immediately vanished from all official records.

CHAPTER NINETEEN

"I would sit in front of the fire and squeeze the peel of the little oranges into the edge of the flame and watch the sputter of blue that they made" Ernest Hemingway

"It's not the years, honey, it's the mileage" Indiana Jones character, Raiders of the Lost Ark

Well that's it for now. Are there more stories to tell? Yes, I think so, a couple anyway. But those are Tales For Another Day. Right now, the dog's asleep and the fire's mostly out.

There is a minor-league baseball team here in Colorado Springs; the Sky Sox. Most every Friday night during our drowsy Colorado summers the Sox play other minor league teams. Their games are usually in the stadium just across the way from our house.

Following each local game is a fireworks display. We watch it, my wife and I, either from the back porch or from our bedroom where the fireworks are perfectly framed by the windows. I have always loved fireworks, but often, watching them, I find myself drifting.

I think of the gunfire in Arkansas the night they tried to kill us and sometimes in the sky against the reds and greens I see a roped bear in a tree. If the fireworks go on long enough, through the bang and crackle I faintly hear Cinderella again threatening to cut my balls off and Vic begging for help as he bled out on the mountain. And though the evenings are warm and smell of cut grass, for some strange reason I am reminded of how cold it was, so very cold in

Hollywood the night we screwed everything up.

When we buried Dad, my brother and I stood looking down into the urn sized hole dug in the frozen South Dakota ground. My brother, who rarely showed any emotion at all, angrily threw down a handful of dirt and cried out "What's the point? What's the point of it all?"

I had no answer for him then and I have no answer for me now.

The closest I have ever been able to come to meaning is the feeling I get sometimes when I look at my wife during those fireworks shrouded evenings. Often we speak of things from our more than four decades together. Usually we smile, occasionally not. Sometimes I just can't help myself; I reach out and take her hand. She is so beautiful.

Note from the Author

Yes, there are a few more Tales to come, for good or ill. If you're so inclined, you can help bring them to life by sharing your review online where able.

If you do so, I would be grateful for a couple of reasons: first, if you think this iteration of Tales sucks and you tell me why, I can improve the next go. Second, if you liked *Tales From The Day* and say it in a review, it will be a real help both with sales and for an authorish keep on, keepin' on. If you would be so kind as do a review, just search for *Tales From The Day* online or where you purchased copy. Once you find the listing (it should pop right up), you can create and leave your review there.

If you would like to contact me directly,
please just email me at
talesfromtheday8@gmail.com
or leave a message on my blog
www.talesfromtheday.com.

Thanks...and remember: we've all got a damn fine story to tell.

Thank you so much for reading one of our **Humor Memoirs**.

If you enjoyed our book, please check out our recommended title for your next great read!

Nazis & Nudists by David Haldane

"Haldane's storytelling is rapid, fact-packed, devoid of filler (and) heavy on action." –*Long Beach Press Telegram*

"The story is unflinching, wildly improbable and pretty scary in spots." –Ken Borgers, *KSDS 88.3 San Diego*

Made in the USA
Middletown, DE
10 April 2019